CREATE YOUR OWN REWARDING RETIREMENT

A Comprehensive Guide for Creating Goals After You Retire

JOSEPH "JAY" TOTTER

outskirts press

Create Your Own Rewarding Retirement
A Comprehensive Guide for Creating Goals After You Retire
All Rights Reserved.
Copyright © 2021 Joseph (Jay) Totter
v1.0

The opinions expressed in this manuscript are solely the opinions of the author and do not represent the opinions or thoughts of the publisher. The author has represented and warranted full ownership and/or legal right to publish all the materials in this book.

This book may not be reproduced, transmitted, or stored in whole or in part by any means, including graphic, electronic, or mechanical without the express written consent of the publisher except in the case of brief quotations embodied in critical articles and reviews.

Outskirts Press, Inc.
http://www.outskirtspress.com

ISBN: 978-1-9772-3040-9

Library of Congress Control Number: 2021900092

Cover Photo © 2021 www.gettyimages.com. All rights reserved - used with permission.

Outskirts Press and the "OP" logo are trademarks belonging to Outskirts Press, Inc.

PRINTED IN THE UNITED STATES OF AMERICA

Contents

Preface i
Introduction iii

Retirement Domains 1

Health Domain Description 3
Chapter 1: Physical 5
Chapter 2: Intellectual 11
Chapter 3: Mental 19
Chapter 4: Emotional 25
Chapter 5: Social 31
Chapter 6: Spiritual 37
Health Domain Goal Example 43
Health Domain Goal Tracking Sheet 45

Wealth Domain Description 47
Chapter 7: Social Security 49
Chapter 8: Pension 57
Chapter 9: Tax-Deferred Accounts 65
Chapter 10: Savings 73
Chapter 11: Investments 81
Chapter 12: Work 89
Wealth Domain Goal Example 97
Wealth Domain Goal Tracking Sheet 99

Self Domain Description 101
Chapter 13: Beliefs 103
Chapter 14: Values 109
Chapter 15: Interests 115
Chapter 16: Self-Image 121
Chapter 17: Family 127
Chapter 18: Goals 135
Self Domain Goal Example 143
Self Domain Goal Tracking Sheet 145

Conclusion 147
References 149

Preface

I am a retired Baby Boomer, just like the other 34 million of us. I retired after 40 years in a public sector education job and within a week was working in my current private sector sales job. It did not happen by chance. It was planned. I knew that it was the right retirement for me after researching my options and talking to plenty of people. During the ensuing years, I discovered that I had missed a lot of information and had not considered a lot of factors which would have enriched my retirement in immeasurable ways. This began a two-year journey of investigation to capture what I had missed and to share that information with those around me in order for them to benefit from my experience. Because of their encouragement, I put pen to paper to create *Discover the Right Retirement for You*, the most comprehensive guide for retirement planning available in the current market.

Following the success of that book, it became apparent that my job was only half done, with the following frequent response from readers: You got me *to* retirement, now get me *through* retirement. Consequently, *Create Your Own Rewarding Retirement* was written for the 78 million Baby Boomers: the 34 million who have already retired and the 44 million who are retiring at an astonishing rate of 10,000 each day, who are searching for guidance to get them through retirement by creating and completing their goals. Market research conducted through interviews of retired Baby Boomers revealed that only about one-third of them were satisfied with their retirement, while the remaining two-thirds of them wanted a retirement that they described as more rewarding. As a follow-up to this response, they were asked the question: "What would help make your retirement a more satisfying journey?" The combined summary of their responses revealed they wanted a *consolidated document* that was *convenient to use* about the *components of retirement* that *contained guidance for creating goals* and *connected them to others* like themselves. Each of these features was incorporated into this book.

Consolidated document was described as one which has everything the reader needs to create their retirement goals brought together and available for use within one book. This interview response resulted in the book you are now reading, which is the most comprehensive guide available in the current market for creating a rewarding retirement based on short- and long-term goals.

Convenient to use was described as a workbook-style document that is logically organized and interactive. This interview response resulted in the basic format of the book, which uses a simple worksheet at the end of each chapter to collect your thoughts and create your own short- and long-term retirement goals.

Components of retirement was described as more than that which are included in the typical retirement articles already available and which frequently report only on the financial aspects without considering other factors like the effect of retirement on self-image, mental health, and the like. This interview response resulted in the model of the three domains of health, wealth, and self, the six associated factors in each domain, and their importance in creating short- and long-term retirement goals.

Contained guidance for creating goals was described as a logical step-by-step process by which the reader could create their own short- and long-term retirement goals. This interview response resulted in the use of the SMART goal format, which emphasizes that such goals should be specific, measurable, achievable, realistic, and timely.

Connected them to others was described as stories about real people just like the reader. This interview response resulted in an interview approach for gathering information from retirees about their previous retirement expectations and their present retirement experiences. In many instances, the differences between retirees who were satisfied with their retirement and those who wanted a more rewarding one were dramatic and noteworthy of report. The text is filled with such stories about people just like you.

This book is designed to be a companion text to *Discover the Right Retirement for You*, in which you will discover the type of retirement that is best for you, if you have not already done so. *Create Your Own Rewarding Retirement* goes beyond that to help you create and complete your short- and long-term goals after you retire. The reader has several choices as to how to use this book. You can use it as a workbook by completing all of the chapter worksheets and creating your short- and long-term retirement goals; or you can use it as a history book to chronicle your journey as you create and complete each goal; or you can use it as a storybook about the retirement expectations and experiences of people just like you. Each of these choices will be of value to you. Ideally, this book is intended to be used in all three ways and it is recommended that you do so in order to achieve the maximum value from it. Remember that you, and you alone, have the ability to make an ordinary retirement into an extraordinary one.

Introduction

Congratulations on your retirement. What type of retirement did you select? Retirement with no work? Phased-in retirement with phased-out work? Retirement with part-time work? Or did you select no retirement with continued work, either by continuing to do what you have been doing for most, if not all of your adult life, or by starting an encore career? Regardless of which type of retirement you selected, it is the right retirement for you.

You are now entering a new phase in your life journey that will last 20 years on average. In many instances it will last a lot longer, with many of you living a retirement life that equals, or even exceeds, the length of your work life. Regardless of the type of retirement you have chosen or how long it lasts, it will be more rewarding if you take charge and create short- and long-term retirement goals as a guide for your daily life. The time will fly by, just like it did when you were working.

The secret to living your own rewarding retirement is by creating short- and long-term goals that can be described using the acronym SMART. *S* refers to specific, *M* refers to measurable, *A* refers to achievable, *R* refers to relevant, and *T* refers to timely. A specific goal is one that includes enough detail to be well defined and unambiguous. A measurable goal is one that has specific criteria by which to measure the progress toward and final accomplishment of the goal. An achievable goal is one that is attainable given your available human and material resources. A realistic goal is one that is relevant and within reach. And lastly, a timely goal is one with a beginning and ending date.

In order to help you with the next phase of your life journey, *Create Your Own Rewarding Retirement* has been designed as a companion text to *Discover the Right Retirement for You*. The eighteen chapters in both books parallel each other, with this book providing a summary of each domain factor, interview results of retiree expectations and experiences, stories of retirees who were satisfied with their retirement and those who wanted a more rewarding one, and three recommended goal areas from which the reader may choose that were the most commonly reported in the interviews. At the end of each chapter is a SMART goal worksheet for creating your own short- or long-term retirement goals.

The possibilities for creating short- and long-term retirement goals are endless. The reader may create a retirement goal for each of the domains, for one or more factors in a specific domain, or any combination thereof among the three domains of health, wealth, and self, and the total of eighteen factors. It is recommended that the reader start small with one short-term retirement goal, build up to more short-term retirement goals, and then expand the process into a sequence of short-term retirement goals to create and complete a more complicated and chronologically longer retirement goal. The process will become easier the more you do it and can be repeated endlessly throughout your entire retirement, no matter how long it may last. The results will amaze you.

The reader should take the following steps toward creating your own rewarding retirement using the information and resources included in this book.

Step 1. Select a domain with which to start followed by the remaining two domains in any order.

Step 2. Read each of the chapters which summarize the six factors of that domain.

Step 3. Refer back to the detailed information about each factor contained in *Discover the Right Retirement for You* if you need to and have not already done so.

Step 4. Complete the one-page SMART retirement goal worksheet at the end of each chapter.

Step 5. Create a short- or long-term SMART retirement goal for each factor as appropriate.

Step 6. Select specific strategies to successfully accomplish the short- or long-term SMART retirement goal and implement them.

Step 7. Revisit the process as often as necessary, as you accomplish each goal or conditions change.

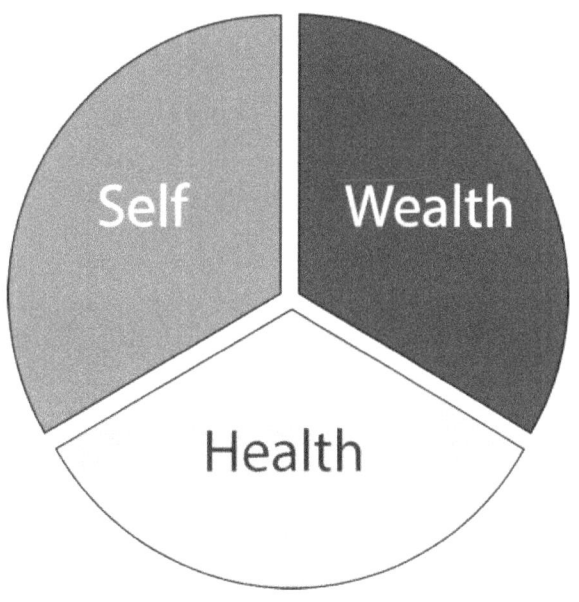

Health Domain

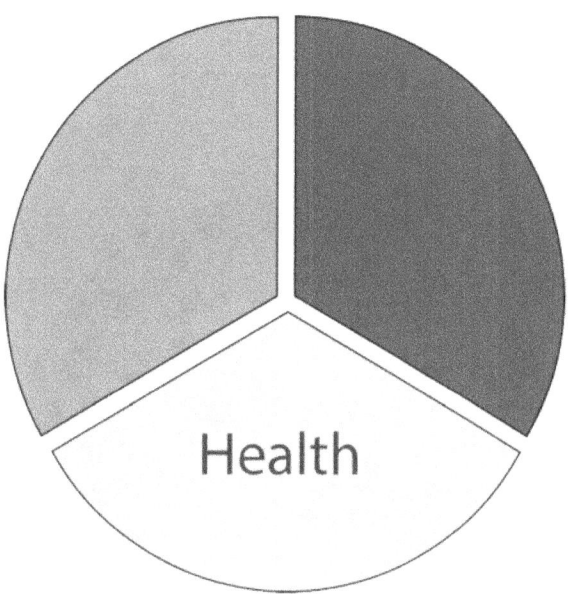

The Health Domain is concerned with all aspects of the individual's well-being from the physical to the psychological. It includes the six factors of physical, intellectual, mental, emotional, social, and spiritual health. The goal is to achieve and maintain a healthy balance between body and mind during the working years, as well as into and throughout retirement regardless of the number of years.

Health Factors

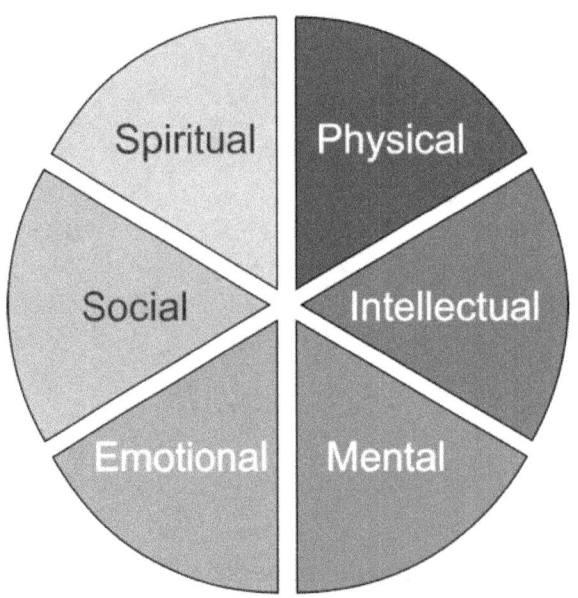

Chapter 1
PHYSICAL

Retirement is a blank sheet of paper. It is a chance to redesign your life into something new and different.
Patrick Foley

The following is a summary of the physical health factor, which was first introduced in *Discover the Right Retirement for You*. The reader may choose to use the following summary, or review the complete description in that book, to create and complete your short- and long-term retirement goals for the physical health factor.

There are natural physical changes that come with aging, regardless of whether you are working or retired. These changes are due to a combination of genetics, or what you inherit from your parents, and lifestyle, or how you live your life. They include changes in your skin, skeletal, muscular, nervous, endocrine, cardiovascular, lymphatic, respiratory, digestive, urinary, and reproductive systems. The changes may occur in only one of these systems, but frequently occur in a number of them, and occasionally, but very rarely, in all of them.

Significant changes also happen to the brain as you grow older due to decreased weight as a result of the loss of brain cells, reduced nerve network, and reduced blood flow carrying oxygen to the brain. This is most noticeable as a change in memory. Reduced sensory input, especially hearing and vision, adds stress as the brain struggles to give meaning to the things that you hear and see. The most common hearing problem is presbycusis, or age-related hearing loss. Many hearing loss problems can be corrected by the use of an amplification device, such as a hearing aid. Consultation with your physician and a referral to an audiologist, or hearing specialist, is recommended. The most common vision problem is presbyopia, or age-related vision loss. Many vision loss problems can be corrected by glasses and contact lenses or through minor surgery. Consultation with your physician and a referral to an ophthalmologist or vision specialist, is recommended.

Many of these physical conditions have an adverse effect on the sleep patterns of retirees. Even though sleep needs remain constant throughout adulthood at about 6½ to 7 hours each night, sleep patterns change with age. Retirees report that they have a more difficult time falling asleep, awaken more frequently during the night, and arise earlier in the morning. If you cannot fall asleep within twenty minutes of going to bed, get out of bed, do some relaxing activity, and then return to bed. If you awaken more frequently during the night due to nocturia, which is the need to urinate, or due to discomfort or pain from chronic long-term illness, consult with your physician. A common remedy for nocturia frequently reported by retirees is the reduction of fluids before going to bed. If you arise early in the morning, get out of bed and start your day. There are always plenty of things to be done. Disruption of sleep patterns may lead to sleep deprivation, which results in decreased cognitive activity and increased confusion. These symptoms are usually reduced or eliminated once you get enough sleep. [1]

Workers interviewed for the previous book were equally divided between those who had a physically demanding job and those who had a more sedentary job. Of interest was that both groups of workers did little to improve their physical well-being through exercise unless they had already been inclined to do so as part of their lifestyle outside the workplace. Workers who had a physically demanding job believed that the exertion on the job was all they needed to stay fit to do the job, while workers who had a more sedentary job did not see the need for any exercise related to their job. A number of workers said that they planned to increase the amount of exercise they did once they retired because they would have the time to do so. This was not the retirement reality. The workers who had retired from a physically demanding job had done nothing to replace the physical exertion on the job. The workers who had retired from a more sedentary job also had done nothing to start an exercise routine.

The importance of exercise is well documented as a method for maintaining physical health as you age. Endurance activities increase your breathing and heart rate. They keep your heart, lungs, and circulatory system healthy and improve your overall fitness, making it easier to do many daily activities. Endurance activities include such things as brisk walking, jogging, and dancing. The simple activity of brisk walking for 30 minutes each day equals about two miles in distance and results in better endurance and weight loss. [2] Strength activities make your muscles stronger. Strength activities include such things as lifting weights, using resistance bands, and bicycling. Balance activities help prevent falls which are a common problem in older adults. Lower-body strength exercise will improve balance and decrease falls. Balance activities include such things as standing marches, single-leg stands, and heel-to-toe walking. Flexibility activities stretch muscles and keep your body limber. They keep your arms, legs, and torso in fluid motion which results in extended reach. Flexibility activities are the most common variation of stretching. Passive stretches are done to you by someone else like a personal trainer, and active stretches you do to yourself, with no external force needed. Dynamic stretches, like warming up to go running, are done before the exercise, while static stretches, like cooling down after the run, are done after the exercise.

Retirees interviewed for the book who were satisfied with the physical health factor in their retirement reported that they were in general good health and had few sleep problems, except for a slight increase in nocturia, which many of them controlled to varying degrees with reduction of fluid intake before going to bed. It is noteworthy that almost all of them reported that they exercised daily, even if it was just brisk walking for 30 minutes or so. They all reported regular physical examinations and follow-up examinations with specialists for age-related hearing and vision loss, as well as other age-related physical health conditions. It is noteworthy that they were optimistic about their ability to maintain good physical health throughout their retirement with the common recommendations to "stay active" and "keep going."

Logan is a good example of a retiree who is satisfied with his physical health in retirement. He is in general good physical health with mild hypertension, controlled with exercise and medication, and hearing loss, controlled with the use of bilateral hearing aids. He jokingly said "I have outlived three doctors already and expect to outlive three more." In defense of these doctors, it should be noted that at the writing of this book they are retired themselves, so Logan did not literally outlive them. He continued daily walks after he retired and increased the distance from two to four miles. His preferred walking time is in the evening after dinner, which he finds relaxing and as part of his nightly routine in preparation for going to bed at 11:00 p.m. after watching the nightly news. Logan did not report any significant sleep problems, except mild nocturia, for which he said that he had to get up at least once during the night to go to the bathroom. He said that he would not change anything about his physical health routine in retirement and expected to continue it indefinitely.

Retirees interviewed for the book who wanted a more rewarding retirement associated with their physical health were asked "What would be the most important physical thing you would change in order to make your retirement more rewarding as you age?" Their responses were significantly similar in that they consistently identified four factors. First, they said that they wanted to be more proactive in monitoring their physical health, including hearing and vision problems, which seemed to "creep up on them" in a gradual and insidious manner. Second, they said they wanted to get involved in a physical activity, but had all kinds of excuses for not going to the gym. This was noteworthy because the focus was always on going to the gym instead of starting a walking routine or some other less rigorous workout routine that did not require going to the gym. Somehow, going to the gym was connected with routine exercise, as if you could not have one without the other. Third, they said they wanted to be able to sleep throughout the night. On average they were getting up three times during the night to go to the bathroom and frequently reported that they were still tired in the morning because of the interrupted sleep patterns. Lastly, and somewhat surprising, was their fixation on memory loss and the fear that it was the beginning of Alzheimer's disease. It should be noted that most memory loss in retirees is the result of aging, not Alzheimer's disease, and should be addressed with a similar level of concern, not the alarm associated with Alzheimer's disease. Memory loss will be reviewed in the next chapter.

Amanda is a good example of a retiree who wants a more rewarding retirement associated with her physical health. There was literally no exercise in her life and she reported "It becomes more and more difficult to do anything the older I get." When asked to elaborate about this response, she said "I can't even do my grocery shopping without having to lean on the shopping cart and the rows seem to get longer and longer every day." She reported "sleepless" nights with frequent bathroom visits and always feeling tired in the morning. A multitude of physical conditions included significant hypertension, diabetes, and weight gain. It should be noted that all of these physical conditions respond well to diet changes and exercise routines. Amanda simply could not bring herself to do either of these and preferred to exclusively rely on medication. Her unwillingness to attempt diet changes and exercise routines, even in small amounts, speaks volumes about her lack of will power to try to make herself physically healthier. The desire was there, but the will was not.

In summary, retirees interviewed for the book who were satisfied with their retirement frequently reported general good health, restful sleep patterns, and regular exercise as represented by the following figure. The reader is encouraged to create a short- or long-term retirement goal in one or more of these areas, if determined to be appropriate after self-reflection, by taking the following steps.

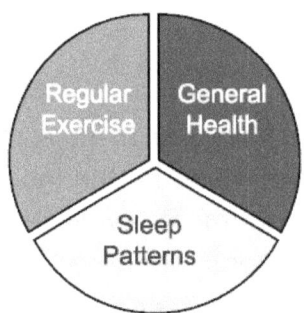

Suggested Topics for Creating a
Physical Health Retirement Goal

- ☐ Review and reflect on the information contained in the chapter.

- ☐ Refer back to the detailed information about the physical health factor contained in *Discover the Right Retirement for You* if you need to and have not already done so.

- ☐ Complete the SMART goal worksheet and compare *My Description of What Is Now* with *My Description of What Will Be*.

- ☐ Create a short- or long-term SMART goal as appropriate.

- ☐ Select specific strategies to successfully accomplish the goal and implement them.

- ☐ Revisit the process as often as necessary, as you accomplish each goal or conditions change.

SMART Goal Worksheet

Domain: *Health*   Factor: *Physical*

Directions: Complete *My Description of What Is Now* and *My Description of What Will Be*. If they match there is nothing to do. If they do not match create a short- or long-term SMART goal including specific strategies to accomplish the goal.

My Description of What Is Now	My Description of What Will Be

SMART Goal
Specific – Measurable – Achievable – Realistic – Timely

I will _____ by _____ as measured by _____ .
        Insert Goal   Insert Date   Insert Measurement

Strategies to Accomplish the SMART Goal

Strategy 1. _____
Strategy 2. _____
Strategy 3. _____

Chapter 2
INTELLECTUAL

Age is a matter of mind over matter. If you don't mind, it doesn't matter.
Mark Twain

The following is a summary of the intellectual health factor, which was first introduced in *Discover the Right Retirement for You*. The reader may choose to use the following summary, or review the complete description in that book, to create and complete your short- and long-term retirement goals for the intellectual health factor.

The concepts of crystallized and fluid intelligence are used to describe the patterns of intellectual, or cognitive change, that occur over a lifetime. Crystallized intelligence refers to the knowledge, abilities, and skills that are familiar and repeatedly practiced, such as vocabulary, and continue to improve into later adult life, peaking at 60 to 70 years of age, on average, before they begin to decline. Consequently, older adults do better on tasks requiring this type of intelligence than do younger adults. This adds credibility to the old adage "with age comes wisdom." Conversely, fluid intelligence refers to the ability to solve problems and reason about things in creative ways that are independent from what one has learned through crystallized intelligence, such as divergent or creative "outside the box" problem-solving, peaking at 30 years of age on average before they begin to decline. Consequently, younger adults do better on tasks requiring this type of intelligence than do older adults.

Fluid intelligence includes attention, processing speed, visuospatial skills, language, executive functioning, and memory. [3] Attention is the ability to focus and concentrate on a specific stimulus. Sustained and selective attention are both needed when you have to focus on one thing at a time. Sustained attention is the ability to focus on one specific task for a continuous amount of time without being distracted. Selective attention is the ability to select from many stimuli and to focus on only the one that you want while filtering out other distractions. Alternating and divided attention are needed when you have to focus on multiple things at the same time. Alternating attention is the ability to shift focus between tasks having different types of cognitive requirements. Divided attention is the ability to respond to two or more different demands simultaneously and it is often referred to as multi-tasking. Attention declines with age and seldom targets just one of the four types previously described. Once an attention problem occurs in one area, it is usually followed by problems in the remaining areas.

Processing speed is the time it takes to recognize a stimulus, process the input, mentally create a response, and complete either the cognitive or physical motor response. The stimulus can be in any of the sensory input channels of audition, vision, tactician tact, olfaction, and gustation. Fast processing speed means that the individual is an efficient thinker, learner, and responder. Slow processing speed means that certain tasks will be more difficult than others and will take more time to complete. The importance of fast processing speed cannot be emphasized enough as the person encounters thousands of stimuli daily coming through all of the sensory input channels and requiring split-second decisions and actions. The brain is further taxed beyond the factor of the sheer number of stimuli because some of the stimuli come into the system in serial fashion, that is, one stimulus followed by the next, while some come into the system in simultaneous fashion, that is, one stimulus on top of another at the same time, but from different sense organs. Slower processing speed inhibits the brain from responding to every stimulus because it takes too much time to respond to the earlier stimulus.

Visuospatial skills are the ability to represent, analyze, and mentally manipulate objects in the real world around you. They assist you in orienting yourself in and moving around the environment, and include depth and distance perception. Visuospatial skills are divided into spatial relationship and spatial visualization. Spatial relationship is the ability to represent and mentally manipulate two-dimensional objects which have height and width. These objects can be seen, but not touched, like looking at a picture of a square. Spatial visualization is the ability to represent and mentally manipulate three-dimensional objects which have height, width, and depth. These objects can be seen and touched, such as handling a wooden cube. Literally every movement we make in the world around us is reliant on visuospatial skills.

Language is a complex brain activity that intertwines crystallized and fluid intelligence. It relies on reception, or the incoming information to the brain, and expression, or outgoing information sent by the brain. Language is an amazing skill that is a combination of many discrete behaviors which interact to create effective and efficient communication. These behaviors are semantics, syntax, prosody, and pragmatics. Semantics refers to the words you use. Syntax refers to how you put the words together. Prosody refers to how smoothly you express your ideas. Pragmatics refers to the overall functional use of language. General language ability remains constant over time, especially in the area of vocabulary, but starting around age 70 two language areas show decline. Visual confrontation, the ability to see a common object and name it, declines and may be related to an overall decline in the ability to recall words in general. Verbal fluency, the ability to perform a mental word search to generate a response, also declines, which results in a halting type of speech pattern filled with uncomfortable pauses. A common complaint of older adults is that they cannot find the right word and circumlocute the conversation until they find a less desirable word to substitute. The person is literally at a loss for words.

Executive functioning is a set of processes that deal with managing oneself in order to get a task completed. It includes a set of brain-based skills commonly related to mental control and self-regulation. Executive functioning includes eight skills. Inhibition is the ability to stop a behavior. Shift is the ability to change from one situation to the next. Emotional control is the ability to bring rational thought to bear on feelings. Initiation is the ability to begin work on a task. Working memory is the ability to hold information in the brain for the purpose of completing a task. Planning is the ability to manage current and future-oriented activities related to the task. Organization is the ability to impose order to the task. Self-monitoring is the ability to monitor one's own performance during the task and match it against an established standard. [4] There are hundreds of tasks to be completed every day. Many of the tasks will not be completed in the absence of even one of the executive functioning skills. Most, if not all of the tasks, will not be completed in the absence of more, if not all, of the executive functioning skills.

Memory problems are a common complaint among older adults. The two types of memory are declarative and non-declarative. Declarative, or explicit memory, is the conscious recollection of facts and events. Declarative memory is further broken down into semantic and episodic memory. Declarative semantic memory involves practical knowledge and language. Declarative episodic memory involves personally experienced events that occur at a specific time and place. Non-declarative, or implicit memory, is outside of the person's conscious awareness, like riding a bicycle. Once you learn how to do it, you never forget.

Memory problems can also be described in terms of the length of time they are held in the brain. Sensory memory is held for only a few seconds and relates to recalling sensory experiences from the five sensory organs. The memory fades away once the person makes their response to the stimulus. Short-term memory is held for up to a few days and relates to recalling information recently given to the person. Long-term memory is held indefinitely and relates to recalling information from throughout the person's life. Memory progresses from sensory to short-term and then to long-term based upon the strength of the relevance of the information. Inconsequential information goes away quickly. Important information stays indefinitely.

There is sufficient research evidence to support the idea that continuing to stay mentally active will slow the intellectual aging process. The advantage of stimulating mental activity, from the daily newspaper crossword puzzle to the more challenging "how to" projects, cannot be overstated.

Retirees interviewed for the book who were satisfied with the intellectual health factor in their retirement reported positive experiences related to both crystallized and fluid intelligence to varying degrees based upon their age. Presented with a closely-scripted interview protocol, they were able to relay many examples of the six components of fluid intelligence with noteworthy accuracy. They were also able to describe what compensatory behaviors they had undertaken to ameliorate, or control the disruption caused by an age-related condition, especially memory loss. These compensatory behaviors included everything from simple lists to more complicated mnemonic devices, which are memory devices that aid information retention and retrieval. These mnemonic devices included the following: visualization, or creating mental pictures; acronyms, or creating a word using the first letter of each item; acrostics, or creating a phrase using each item; acoustics, or creating a "sing-song" rhyme; and chunking, or creating smaller, more manageable bits of information from larger ones.

Ramona is a good example of a retiree who is satisfied with her intellectual health in retirement. Her self-reported profile reflects the expected changes in crystallized and fluid intelligence for a woman who is 72 years of age. The most notable feature is some memory loss. Her speech pattern was slightly halting during her interview as she searched for the right words to say, but it was not so impaired as to cause either her or the interviewer concern. She said that she is a "lister" and needs to make lists so as not to forget things of importance. It was also noteworthy that she accepted being a "lister" as a result of her age and that the compensatory strategy of making lists was "perfectly normal for a woman my age."

Retirees interviewed for the book who wanted a more rewarding retirement associated with their intellectual health were highly animated and obvious about their intellectual performance and wanted to improve it because of the difficulties it imposed on their daily lives. Especially noteworthy was the presence of problems in most, if not all of the six components of fluid intelligence, with more components being involved as the severity increased. Every retiree interviewed spoke to one or more of the fluid intelligence components of attention, processing speed, visuospatial skills, language, executive functioning, and memory difficulties. Some had difficulties in only a few, while others had difficulties in all of them. The most frequent difficulty reported was that of memory. A troubling profile emerged of retirees who were frustrated with their memory problems but who took no specific actions, like making lists, to ameliorate their condition. Unlike retirees who were satisfied with the intellectual health factor in their retirement and who had done something about it, these retirees expressed obvious concern without doing anything about it. Complaining about it and doing something to fix it are worlds apart.

Gloria is a good example of a retiree who wants a more rewarding retirement associated with her intellectual health. She described difficulties in all six of the fluid intelligence components to varying degrees. The most frightening was with her processing speed and visuospatial skills as related to her struggles with driving at age 76. She recalled a number of "minor" car accidents, as she described them, which were way too frequent for comfort. "The DMV still renews my driver's license, so they must know what they are doing" was her response when asked if she was concerned about the number of car accidents. She brought up memory difficulties a number of times, but had no strategies with which to cope with them. Her subtle call for help was apparent when she asked the interviewer if he knew if any of the other retirees who were interviewed had similar memory problems and what they said they did to improve their memory.

In summary, retirees interviewed for the book who were satisfied with their retirement were able to give positive and well-articulated examples of crystallized and fluid intelligence, as well as evidence of successful memory capabilities as represented by the following figure. The reader is encouraged to create a short- or long-term retirement goal in one or more of these areas, if determined to be appropriate after self-reflection, by taking the following steps.

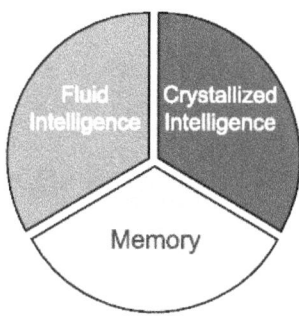

Suggested Topics for Creating an
Intellectual Health Retirement Goal

☐ Review and reflect on the information contained in the chapter.

☐ Refer back to the detailed information about the intellectual health factor contained in *Discover the Right Retirement for You* if you need to and have not already done so.

☐ Complete the SMART goal worksheet and compare *My Description of What Is Now* with *My Description of What Will Be*.

☐ Create a short- or long-term SMART goal as appropriate.

☐ Select specific strategies to successfully accomplish the goal and implement them.

☐ Revisit the process as often as necessary, as you accomplish each goal or conditions change.

SMART Goal Worksheet

Domain: *Health*   Factor: *Intellectual*

Directions: Complete *My Description of What Is Now* and *My Description of What Will Be*. If they match there is nothing to do. If they do not match create a short- or long-term SMART goal including specific strategies to accomplish the goal.

My Description of What Is Now	My Description of What Will Be

SMART Goal

Specific – Measurable – Achievable – Realistic – Timely

I will _____ by _____ as measured by _____.
       Insert Goal   Insert Date   Insert Measurement

Strategies to Accomplish the SMART Goal

Strategy 1. _____
Strategy 2. _____
Strategy 3. _____

Chapter 3
MENTAL

It's paradoxical that the idea of living a long life appeals to everyone, but the idea of getting old doesn't appeal to anyone.
Andy Rooney

The following is a summary of the mental health factor, which was first introduced in *Discover the Right Retirement for You*. The reader may choose to use this summary, or review the complete description in that book, to create and complete your short- and long-term retirement goals for the mental health factor.

The World Health Organization (WHO) has defined mental health as "… a state of well-being in which every individual realizes his or her own potential, can cope with the normal stresses of life, can work productively and fruitfully, and is able to make a contribution to his or her community." [5]

People who are mentally healthy can cope with the normal stresses of life by shaping the environment around them, which is an active behavior, or adjusting to it, which is a more passive behavior. Many retirees report that they still have stress in their personal life, but it is significantly reduced after leaving the daily work routine. They report that they deal with stress in general ways, but do not directly deal with the situation that causes it. Addressing one, but not the other, is not productive. You either have to change the situation or change your reaction to the situation when dealing with stress.

The National Mental Health Association (NMHA) has identified the ten positive behaviors of people who are mentally healthy. [6] It is important to learn more about these behaviors and to determine if they exist at home once you have retired since the stress attributed to work has been eliminated.

First, people who are mentally healthy feel good about themselves. They like who they have become as a result of their life experiences and look forward to continued growth. Second, people who are mentally healthy do not become overwhelmed by their emotions. It is only natural that your emotions get the best of you sometimes. Put your emotions in perspective in relation to the rest of your life. Third, people who are mentally healthy have satisfying personal relationships. A satisfying personal relationship is based on trust, mutual respect, mindfulness, diversity, and communication. Open and honest communication is the most important of these features. Fourth, people who are mentally healthy feel comfortable with other people. Everyone feels awkward sometimes, but we are surrounded by people all day long, which requires various levels of social interaction focused on effective and efficient communication. Fifth, people who are mentally healthy can laugh at themselves and others. To be able to laugh at yourself, you have to turn down the narcissism, or the excessive interest in or need for admiration of oneself, and turn up the healthy self-interest, or search for the good in oneself. Sixth, people who are mentally healthy have respect for themselves and others. Self-discovery of what things make you respect yourself leads to an understanding of who you are and who you are not. Living a life that is genuine is the essential factor here. Seventh, people who are mentally healthy are able to accept life's disappointments. If you cannot change the outcome of a situation, you have to accept the disappointment and move on. Eighth, people who are mentally healthy can meet life's demands and handle problems when they arise. There is a lesson to be learned in every problem. Go out and learn the lesson and then go on with your life. Ninth, people who are mentally healthy make their own decisions. Unless an immediate decision is needed, it is wise to seek advice, take it under consideration, add your gut instinct, make a decision, and take action. And lastly, people who are mentally healthy shape the environment around them or adjust to it. In order to change the situation, try avoiding the stressor if it is not of significant importance or alter the situation so it does not reoccur in the future. In order to change your reaction to the situation, try to adapt to the stressor by changing your attitude and expectations or by accepting the things that you cannot change.

Retirees interviewed for the book who were satisfied with the mental health factor in their retirement confirmed that they still had stress in their life, but it was significantly reduced after leaving the daily work routine. They reported that they believed their retirement was productive and approximately one-third of them reported that they were making a contribution to the community, with the examples almost exclusively described as some type of volunteer work. These retirees often spoke of being fortunate with the retirement they had and wanting "to give something back to those who were less fortunate than they were." Time was taken to conduct an extended interview of these retirees with special attention paid to the ten positive behaviors of people who are mentally healthy. A retiree who was satisfied with the mental health factor in their retirement had at least eight of the ten positive behaviors on average. As a group they were overwhelmingly rich in positive mental health behaviors.

Marcus is a good example of a retiree who is satisfied with the mental health factor in his retirement. He reported nine of the ten positive behaviors on his extended interview and was able to give well-articulated and vividly rich examples for each behavior. It was enjoyable to interview him because he was so engaging and positive. It was noteworthy that he felt that he was not contributing enough to the community and had been making plans to extend his volunteer services to a second local food bank. When asked how he handles life's disappointments, he responded by saying "I roll with the punches. That's all there is to it."

Retirees interviewed for the book who wanted a more rewarding retirement associated with their mental health were all over the place in relationship to the ten positive behaviors of people who are mentally healthy. Time was taken to conduct an extended interview of these retirees with special attention paid to the ten positive behaviors of people who are mentally healthy. A retiree who wanted a more rewarding retirement had fewer than two of the ten positive behaviors on average. As a group they were noticeably poor in positive mental health behaviors.

Martha is a good example of a retiree who wants a more rewarding retirement associated with her mental health. Even though she was in the extreme range of this group of retirees, it is important to share her story because it is exemplary of what a negative mental health factor can do to a person. She was unable to present any relationship, even with her own family, that could be described as personally satisfying. She was awkward during the interview, with short responses, and the interview seemed to cause her an elevated level of stress. She was asked three times if she wanted to stop the interview as a result of her obvious discomfort, but she declined to do so. It was evident that she was conflicted between wanting to do the interview and have some amount of attention, but being uneasy about it and unable to effectively communicate with the interviewer. She was unable to provide even one example for any of the ten positive behaviors of people who are mentally healthy. It is believed that she will have a very difficult time trying to improve her mental health, and consequently her retirement, even with professional help.

In summary, retirees interviewed for the book who were satisfied with their retirement frequently reported that they were able to successfully cope with stress, work productively, and contribute to their community as represented by the following figure. The reader is encouraged to create a short- or long-term retirement goal in one or more of these areas, if determined to be appropriate following your self-reflection, by taking the following steps.

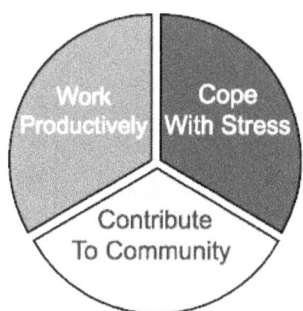

Suggested Topics for Creating a
Mental Health Retirement Goal

☐ Review and reflect on the information contained in the chapter.

☐ Refer back to the detailed information about the mental health factor contained in *Discover the Right Retirement for You* if you need to and have not already done so.

- ☐ Complete the SMART goal worksheet and compare *My Description of What Is Now* with *My Description of What Will Be.*

- ☐ Create a short- or long-term SMART goal as appropriate.

- ☐ Select specific strategies to successfully accomplish the goal and implement them.

- ☐ Revisit the process as often as necessary, as you accomplish each goal or conditions change.

SMART Goal Worksheet

Domain: *Health* Factor: *Mental*

Directions: Complete *My Description of What Is Now* and *My Description of What Will Be*. If they match there is nothing to do. If they do not match create a short- or long-term SMART goal including specific strategies to accomplish the goal.

My Description of What Is Now	My Description of What Will Be

SMART Goal
Specific – Measurable – Achievable – Realistic – Timely

I will _____ by _____ as measured by _____.
       Insert Goal   Insert Date   Insert Measurement

Strategies to Accomplish the SMART Goal

Strategy 1. _____
Strategy 2. _____
Strategy 3. _____

Chapter 4
EMOTIONAL

I am not giving in to anyone else's idea of how I ought to feel and look at 70. Retirement is not a world I can even visualize. I retire when I go to bed.
Carmen Dell Orefice

The following is a summary of the emotional health factor, which was first introduced in *Discover the Right Retirement for You.* The reader may choose to use the following summary, or review the complete description in that book, to create and complete your short- and long-term retirement goals for the emotional health factor.

The terms "mental health" and "emotional health" are sometimes used interchangeably. Mental health refers to a continuum of feelings, thoughts, and behaviors from the positive to the pathologic, often referred to as mental illness. Emotional health is an extension of mental health and refers to the way in which someone views and lives a life of wellness. Even though the distinction may seem to be minor, it is an important one. This is the reason for devoting separate chapters in the book to mental and emotional health.

There are eight primary emotions. These emotions are wired into your brain when you are born. An example of a primary emotion is anger. There are secondary emotions, or responses in reaction to a primary emotion. An example of a secondary emotion is a feeling of regret when you get angry. There are also plenty of other emotions, which are learned from our families and connected to our culture, which are unique to the individual. These are referred to esoteric emotions.

Improving emotional health is similar to improving physical health. It transcends the notion of the mere freedom from illness to involve actively feeling and living well. Emotional health and well-being involve defining and creating your own life worth living. An important step in creating emotional health is to identify your own emotions and to understand their value. All emotions have meaning simply because they are part of who you are and how you react to situations. They are inescapable in your daily life. The goal is to develop emotional intelligence (EI), which is the ability to recognize when an emotion is occurring, identify the emotion, and use it constructively in the situation. This leads to emotional regulation (ER), which is the ability to control and monitor your emotions by adjusting your mindset and behavior accordingly. [7]

A brief review of the eight primary emotions is warranted. Anger is the emotion characterized by antagonism, usually in the form of passive or active aggression toward someone or something you feel has deliberately done you wrong. Sadness is the emotion characterized by a transient mood or unhappy feeling and is a great motivator. You want to stay where you are doing what you are doing when you are happy, but you want to change all of that when you are sad. Fear is the emotion characterized by the belief that someone or something is dangerous, likely to cause you harm, or a threat. It is a powerful, primitive emotion that alerts you to either real or perceived danger with the physical reaction of "flight-fight-freeze." Joy is the emotion characterized by a range of feelings from contentment and satisfaction to bliss and intense pleasure. Joy and happiness are often used interchangeably, but they are very different things. Joy comes from an internal feeling of being at peace with oneself, but happiness comes externally from other people, things, and events. Interest is the emotion characterized by focusing your attention to varying degrees on a person, object, or event. The greater the interest, the greater the focused attention. Surprise is the emotion characterized by a sense of astonishment, wonder, or amazement that is caused by something sudden or unexpected. The response to surprise ranges from subtle to intense and from positive to negative. An example of a subtle positive surprise is the unexpected "thinking of you" card you receive from a friend whom you have not seen for a few months. It is pleasant, but there is minimal impact. An example of an intense negative surprise is the person jumping when a balloon is popped. There is a maximum physical response to the loud noise. Disgust is the emotion characterized by a strong negative feeling often accompanied by exaggerated facial expressions and guttural sounds like "ach" and "ugh." The response is one of rejection or revulsion toward something potentially contagious or something considered offensive, distasteful, or unpleasant. And lastly, shame is the emotion characterized by an internal state of inadequacy or unworthiness that makes you feel that there is something basically wrong with yourself. Many times it manifests itself in mortification or an intense feeling of embarrassment.

The National Institutes of Health (NIH) have created a program that includes six strategies for improving your emotional health. [8] First, brighten your outlook on life. People who are emotionally healthy have fewer negative emotions in general and are able to bounce back from difficult situations faster. This characteristic is referred to as resiliency. Second, reduce stress. People who are emotionally healthy use a variety of positive behaviors to actively reduce the stress in their lives. Third, get enough sleep. People who are emotionally healthy get at least 6½ to 7 hours of sleep each night and awake rested and ready to start a new day with its many challenges. Fourth, live a mindful life. People who are emotionally healthy are aware of what is going on internally and externally at the moment, instead of being on autopilot. Fifth, cope with loss. People who are emotionally healthy can successfully work through the five stages of the grieving process when they experience loss. And lastly, strengthen social connections. People who are emotionally healthy have meaningful relationships with family, friends, colleagues, and co-workers.

Retirees interviewed for the book who were satisfied with the emotional health factor in their retirement all shared one noteworthy characteristic. They were all overwhelmingly positive. The interview protocol asked each retiree to respond separately and specifically to the six strategies for improving their emotional health. A consistent pattern emerged in which one positive strategy gave support to another positive strategy and so on. If the retiree had one, they not only had a few more, but invariably had all six strategies. The pattern was unmistakable. An additional interview question probed this pattern and Mark summed it up by saying "Positive gets positive, but you have to work at it."

Matthew is a good example of a retiree who is satisfied with his emotional health in retirement. His interview responses were positive for all six of the strategies for improving emotional health. Some of his interview responses were particularly pointed and poignant, and three are especially noteworthy of report here. In response to the interview question "Do you have a bright outlook on life?" he responded by saying "I grew up in a pitifully dysfunctional family living in poverty and I am thankful every day for just being an average middle-class guy who was able to go to work and pay his bills. My retirement is like a bonus for me and I enjoy every minute of it." In response to the interview question "Do you live a mindful life?" he responded by saying "I like who I am and where I am in my life right now. My only regret is that I wish it would have happened a little bit earlier, but it is what it is." And lastly, in response to the interview question "Do you do things to cope with loss?" he responded by saying "I lost my wife to cancer a few years ago. It was terrible the way she suffered at the end. I was glad that I was able to be there for her every moment until it [her death] happened. I miss her a lot, but I was able to go on with my life after I got over the feeling of emptiness when she died. She would have wanted it that way." What an extraordinary example of someone with positive emotional health.

Retirees interviewed for the book who wanted a more rewarding retirement associated with their emotional health were more scattered in their responses to the six strategies for improving it. None of the retirees were able to speak positively about all of the six strategies and their positive responses varied in degree from casual affirmation to more explicit positive statements. Unlike the retirees who were satisfied with the emotional health factor in their retirement and overwhelmingly spoke in positive terms, these retirees were far more reserved and had numerous negative responses about people, places, and events. The responses for both types of retirees were similar in that they were both explicit, but obviously more consistently positive for one group as opposed to being more consistently negative for the other group.

Samantha is a good example of a retiree who wants a more rewarding retirement associated with her emotional health and who is at the extreme end of the continuum of interviewed retirees. She responded with tepid statements to each of the interview questions related to the six strategies for improving emotional health. The only interview question which resulted in a mildly positive response was when she was asked "Do you work at building social connections?" to which she answered that she had a number of friends with whom she regularly interacted. Of the six strategies for improving emotional health, five of them are more closely associated with actions which could be undertaken privately by the retiree, while only one of them, the building of social connections, requires the direct participation of others. When asked if she desired to have a more robust emotional health, she said she did, but she did not know how to go about doing it. Samantha is a good candidate for professional help.

In summary, retirees interviewed for the book who were satisfied with their retirement affirmed that they had a bright outlook on life, lived a mindful life, coped successfully with loss, had strong social connections, reduced stress, and got enough sleep. Since social connectedness, reduced stress, and getting enough sleep are addressed in other chapters of the book, the reader is encouraged to create a short- or long-term retirement goal in one or more of the remaining three areas, if determined to be appropriate after self-reflection, by taking the following steps.

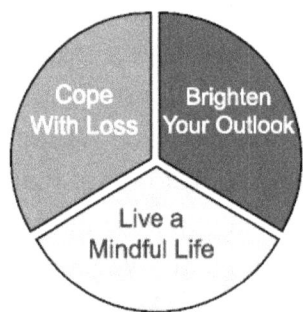

Suggested Topics for Creating an
Emotional Health Retirement Goal

☐ Review and reflect on the information contained in the chapter.

☐ Refer back to the detailed information about the emotional health factor contained in *Discover the Right Retirement for You* if you need to and have not already done so.

☐ Complete the SMART goal worksheet and compare *My Description of What Is Now* with *My Description of What Will Be.*

☐ Create a short- or long-term SMART goal as appropriate.

☐ Select specific strategies to successfully accomplish the goal and implement them.

☐ Revisit the process as often as necessary, as you accomplish each goal or conditions change.

SMART Goal Worksheet

Domain: *Health* **Factor:** *Emotional*

Directions: Complete *My Description of What Is Now* and *My Description of What Will Be*. If they match there is nothing to do. If they do not match create a short- or long-term SMART goal including specific strategies to accomplish the goal.

My Description of What Is Now	My Description of What Will Be

SMART Goal

Specific – Measurable – Achievable – Realistic – Timely

I will _____ by _____ as measured by _____.
         Insert Goal   Insert Date   Insert Measurement

Strategies to Accomplish the SMART Goal

Strategy 1. _____
Strategy 2. _____
Strategy 3. _____

Chapter 5
SOCIAL

Aging seems to be the only available way to live a long life.
Kitty O'Neill Collins

The following is a summary of the social health factor, which was first introduced in *Discover the Right Retirement for You*. The reader may choose to use this summary, or review the complete description in that book, to create and complete your short- and long-term retirement goals for the social health factor.

The World Health Organization (WHO) defines health in general as "… a state of complete physical, mental, and social well-being and not merely the absence of disease or infirmity." Social health is defined as "… the ability to form meaningful relationships with others and act in healthy, positive ways." [9] The way a person connects to the people around them, adapts to different social situations, and experiences a sense of belonging all contribute to social health.

Social connectedness is the measure of how people come together and interact. At an individual level, social connectedness involves the number and quality of connections one has with others in their social circle, including family, friends, colleagues, and co-workers. It goes beyond these individual connections to include the community at large, which is often referred to as community cohesion, and provides positive benefits for both the individual and the community. The benefits of high social connectedness include increased longevity, enhanced illness immunity, and improved emotional regulation skills. The dangers of low social connectedness include susceptibility to anxiety and depression, slower recovery from illness, and increased antisocial behavior.

Social situation adaptability is the manner in which people perceive themselves and proceed with changing their interactions in response to that perception. We are not born with perceptions about ourselves, but rather they develop through our interactions with others, which ultimately influence the overall development of our self-concept and self-esteem. Robert C. Ziller identifies five theories related to the development of our self-concept and self-esteem. [10] The looking glass theory states that how we perceive ourselves comes from our perception of how others see us, and when our self-concept is similar to that of others, we feel socially accepted and well-adjusted. The labeling theory states that how we see ourselves comes from the labels which are placed upon us by others, and we adopt these labels into our self-concept. The social comparison theory states that when we compare ourselves to others, the impact can either be upward—that is, we feel positive because we perceive that we are better than they are—or downward—that is, we feel negative because we perceive that we are not better than they are. The social identity theory states that our sense of self is influenced by the groups to which we belong. And lastly, the self-presentation theory states that how effectively we present ourselves to different social audiences increases our self-esteem if we are successful or decreases it if we are not.

Social belongingness is the sense of being connected to significant, positive, and lasting interpersonal relationships with family, friends, colleagues, co-workers, and members of other groups. Human beings have an almost universal need to form and maintain at least some degree of interpersonal relationship with other human beings. We also have an inherent need to be accepted by a group and by an increasing number of groups as we grow older. We are born into our first group, which is our family. It does not take much energy because it just happens. With it comes a sense of stability and security offered by family members in a long-term relationship—in this case, a lifetime. We choose to belong to other groups outside the family. This takes a lot more energy because we have to approach the group, explore its benefits, decide if the benefits are worth it, and then work at establishing and maintaining the connection.

Retirees interviewed for the book who were satisfied with the social health factor in their retirement consistently confirmed that they had a significant number and variety of social interactions on a regular basis, which they described as being positively connected with others. The examples they described were clearly aligned with the descriptions of social connectedness, social situation adaptability, and social belongingness, although they may not have described them in these exact terms. It was noteworthy that when one of the conditions was present, the remaining two were also consistently present, giving rise to the assumption that social health may occur as a combination of these three conditions and that certain social interactions foster more than one condition simultaneously. The defining lines between social connectedness, social adaptability, and social belongingness were slightly blurred as described by the retirees, but not problematic, because all of them seemed to work together in unison. It was even more interesting that very few of the retirees reported the presence of only one of the conditions in isolation. It was also noteworthy that female retirees were more open about and willing to talk about their social health than were male retirees.

Patricia is a good example of a retiree who is satisfied with the social health factor in her retirement. She has a number of lifelong personal friends with whom she meets on a regular basis for a variety of social activities. She described herself as being socially connected to these friends and felt a strong feeling of belonging to a defined group of friends. She described her social situation adaptability as being able to have fun no matter what her friends decided to do. It was noteworthy that she said "My friends are my security blanket and I can rely on them to be there whenever I need them."

Retirees interviewed for the book who wanted a more rewarding retirement associated with their social health described a deficit in their social interactions. Contrary to the retirees interviewed for the book who were satisfied with their retirement, these retirees almost universally described a life that was devoid of any examples of social connectedness. If this condition was present, it was expressed in a limited fashion with little elaboration and enthusiasm. If social connectedness was not present, or present to a limited degree, the other two social components of social situation adaptability and social belongingness were seldom, if at all, present. As with the retirees who were satisfied with their retirement, female retirees interviewed for the book who wanted a more rewarding retirement were more open about and more willing to talk about their social health than were male retirees.

Florence is a good example of a retiree who wants a more rewarding retirement associated with her social health. Most of her friends were co-workers who drifted away after she retired, because their connection was almost exclusively at work, with few social activities outside the workplace. She had not fostered social interactions beyond those that occurred naturally at work, so she became socially isolated in retirement since her co-workers were gone. She said that she would like to make some new friends, but she was unsure as to how to do that. This situation is complicated by the fact that she described herself as an introvert and she does not have the skills to actively pursue new social interactions outside of immediate family members.

In summary, retirees interviewed for the book who were satisfied with their retirement frequently reported positive feelings about their social connectedness, social situation adaptability, and social belongingness, as represented by the following figure. The reader is encouraged to create a short- or long-term retirement goal in one or more of these areas, if determined to be appropriate following your self-reflection, by taking the following steps.

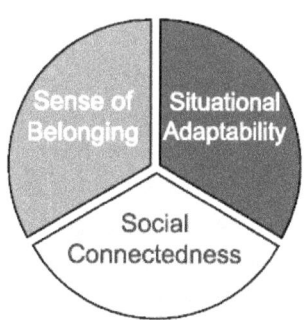

Suggested Topics for Creating a
Social Health Retirement Goal

- ☐ Review and reflect on the information contained in the chapter.

- ☐ Refer back to the detailed information about the social health factor contained in *Discover the Right Retirement for You* if you need to and have not already done so.

- ☐ Complete the SMART goal worksheet and compare *My Description of What Is Now* with *My Description of What Will Be.*

- ☐ Create a short- or long-term SMART goal as appropriate.

- ☐ Select specific strategies to successfully accomplish the goal and implement them.

- ☐ Revisit the process as often as necessary, as you accomplish each goal or conditions change.

SMART Goal Worksheet

Domain: *Health*   Factor: *Social*

Directions: Complete *My Description of What Is Now* and *My Description of What Will Be*. If they match there is nothing to do. If they do not match create a short- or long-term SMART goal including specific strategies to accomplish the goal.

My Description of What Is Now	My Description of What Will Be

SMART Goal
Specific – Measurable – Achievable – Realistic – Timely

I will _____ by _____ as measured by _____.
         Insert Goal   Insert Date   Insert Measurement

Strategies to Accomplish the SMART Goal

Strategy 1. _____
Strategy 2. _____
Strategy 3. _____

Chapter 6
SPIRITUAL

Stay young at heart, kind in spirit, and enjoy retirement living.
Danielle Duckery

The following is a summary of the spiritual factor, which was first introduced in *Discover the Right Retirement for You.* The reader may choose to use this summary, or review the complete description in that book, to create and complete your short- and long-term retirement goals for the spiritual health factor.

Mention the words "spiritual health" and they conjure up a whole host of stereotypical responses, frequently including references to religion and a superior being. The World Health Organization (WHO) defines health as "… a state of complete physical, mental, and social well-being and not merely the absence of disease or infirmity." Its members have been debating the inclusion of spiritual health in the definition under the social domain because of its recognized impact on a person's overall health and happiness. As of the writing of this book, the WHO has not made a decision about the inclusion of spiritual health as part of the definition, but their recognition of its importance and impact is encouraging.

The terms "spiritual" and "religious" are often used synonymously, but there are significant differences between them. Spirituality refers to a person's relationship with transcendent questions, or those questions that go beyond the mere physical human experience, and that confront one as a human being about the meaning and purpose of life. It does not always include an affirmation of a superior being. This relationship is a very personal one and usually not shared with others in an overt and organized fashion. Religion refers to a set of beliefs and practices by a community that usually involves an affirmation of a superior being. This relationship is both personal and institutionalized through an organized group of similar believers. It is possible for a person to be spiritual without being religious. Unfortunately, it is also possible for a person to be religious without being spiritual.

A key concept of spirituality is kindness, which is the quality of being friendly, generous, and considerate. Kindness is the interpersonal, or between people, aspect of spirituality; and spirituality is the overarching intrapersonal, or within oneself, concept. Kindness is one of the external and observable expressions of spirituality. Doing kind deeds is important, but knowing that you are doing them for a higher purpose is even more important. It is recommended that you look around, see where kindness is needed, and then do the kind deed without expectation of recognition or reward. Doing kind deeds has both a figurative and literal effect on your heart and health. Doing kind deeds figuratively and mentally gives you a happy heart, while you literally and physically feel good because of the reduction in stress and other such conditions.

There has been significant attention paid to workplace spirituality over the past few decades. Kent Rhodes [11] reported as early as 2006 that "Though initially the topic of spirituality in the workplace may have been viewed as a passing fad, it now seems to have reached trend status. Identifying desired characteristics of spiritual workplaces can bring us closer to understanding the role that spirituality can play in organizations, the way it can function to positively impact the bottom line, and the value it might bring to members of the work community."

He has identified six components of workplace spirituality which have an impact on the individual worker and are noteworthy when considering retirement. First, it emphasizes sustainability, or the concept that a well-organized business plan identifies potential long-term implications that may have a negative effect on the business and takes action to reduce these risks. Second, it values contribution, or the concept that a business has the responsibility to contribute to the betterment of their community and the world. Third, it prizes creativity, or the concept that as technology, demographics, and market changes happen, a business must creatively rethink its products and services. Fourth, it cultivates inclusion, or the concept that all workers bring their beliefs, values, skills, and unique life experiences to the workplace. Fifth, it develops principles, or the concept that there are benefits to embracing the whole person at work by promoting professional growth while also promoting personal growth. And lastly, it promotes vocation, or the concept of a strong feeling that the work you are doing is important.

Retirees interviewed for the book who were satisfied with the spiritual health factor in their retirement consistently reported that they lived by spiritual principles, often describing these as a "Do unto others as you would have them do unto you" approach to life. The overwhelming majority of them said that they were regular church-goers who also participated in other church related activities, such a Bible study, and the like. This response was expected because of the close connection between spirituality and religion. Every retiree interviewed said that they regularly did kind deeds and the examples they provided were rich with detail. The significance that these kind deeds brought to the lives of the retirees cannot be overstated.

Helen is a good example of a retiree who is satisfied with the spirituality factor in her retirement. She attends church weekly and actively participates in many other church activities, including being on the board overseeing the church building fund. She connects her spirituality with her religious practices and sees them as inseparable. Helen's retirement is filled with many volunteer activities, including weekly activities at the local library and hospital. During the interview she said that her expression of spirituality was nurtured by her parents as a way of life and that she would not live her life in any other way. She was particularly verbal when offering examples of the many kind deeds she has done, and her face literally lit up when describing certain experiences. It was particularly noteworthy when she said "You just have to look around to see so many people who need your help. It looks different every time. My motto is just to do it and not make a big thing about it."

Retirees interviewed for the book who wanted a more rewarding retirement associated with their spiritual health varied considerably in the expression of their spirituality, with the profile of a few of them even looking like that of Helen in the previous paragraph. However, the typical profile was that of an individual who exclusively spoke about their spirituality as a religious experience. It was noteworthy that all of them reported deeds of kindness, which varied considerably in their expression regardless of their description of spirituality and religion. The other outstanding difference was in the frequency of their occurrence, with far fewer deeds of kindness reported than those reported by the retirees who were satisfied with their retirement. Whereas retirees who were satisfied with their retirement reported almost daily deeds of kindness, the retirees who wanted a more rewarding retirement reported far fewer such deeds of kindness, with a notable lack of spontaneity. It was almost as if they had to plan deeds of kindness instead of just doing them as they came along.

Thomas is a good example of a retiree who wants a more rewarding retirement associated with his spiritual health. He also attends church weekly like Helen, but does not participate in other church activities. He defines his spirituality exclusively as his attendance at Sunday Mass, even though his spirituality may be deeper than that. Unfortunately, the interview process did not allow for the collection of that type of additional information. When asked about deeds of kindness, he was eager to agree that he does such deeds, but his examples were few and far between. When asked about deeds of kindness he had experienced in the last few weeks, the only example was a donation that he had made to a housing fund for the homeless. It was apparent that his kind deeds had to be more concrete and substantial for him to recognize them as such.

In summary, retirees who were satisfied with their retirement frequently reported that they lived by spiritual principles, participated in religious practices, and performed acts of kindness as represented by the following figure. The reader is encouraged to create a short- and long-term retirement goal in one or more of these areas, if determined to be appropriate following your self-reflection, by taking the following the steps.

Suggested Topics for Creating a
Spiritual Health Retirement Goal

- ☐ Review and reflect on the information contained in this chapter.

- ☐ Refer back to the detailed information about the spiritual factor contained in *Discover the Right Retirement for You* if you need to and have not already done so.

- ☐ Complete the SMART goal worksheet and compare *My Description of What Is Now* with *My Description of What Will Be.*

- ☐ Create a short- or long-term SMART goal as appropriate.

- ☐ Select specific strategies to successfully accomplish the goal and implement them.

- ☐ Revisit the process as often as necessary, as you accomplish each goal or conditions change.

SMART Goal Worksheet

Domain: *Health* Factor: *Spiritual*

Directions: Complete *My Description of What Is Now* and *My Description of What Will Be*. If they match there is nothing to do. If they do not match create a short- or long-term SMART goal including specific strategies to accomplish the goal.

My Description of What Is Now	My Description of What Will Be

SMART Goal
Specific – Measurable – Achievable – Realistic – Timely

I will _____ by _____ as measured by _____.
         Insert Goal   Insert Date   Insert Measurement

Strategies to Accomplish the SMART Goal

Strategy 1. _____
Strategy 2. _____
Strategy 3. _____

SMART Goal Worksheet (Example 1)

Domain: *Health*   Factor: *Physical*

Directions: Complete *My Description of What Is Now* and *My Description of What Will Be*. If they match there is nothing to do. If they do not match create a short- or long-term SMART goal including specific strategies to accomplish the goal.

My Description of What Is Now	My Description of What Will Be
I retired from a desk job and did very little exercise even when I was working. I never really got into the gym routine because I am not a pumping iron kind of guy and I never did understand how driving to the gym to exercise made any sense. The company had a lunchtime walking group that I enjoyed because I could just walk around the neighborhood. My walks were no more than 2 miles and I could set my own pace. I fell into a bad habit once I retired and stopped taking regular walks. I do not feel very healthy and have gained a lot of weight.	I want to feel healthy and loose the weight I have gained. My weight loss target is 25 pounds. I think I can do it through a regular routine of daily walking 3 miles at a brisk pace. There are plenty of hiking trails from which to choose near my house or I can just walk around the neighborhood. My wife has expressed an interest in also walking to loose some extra weight she has gained, so I am going to plan to do it with her. I can extend the length of my walks as my strength increases.

SMART Goal

Specific – Measurable – Achievable – Realistic – Timely

I will *walk 3 miles every day at a brisk pace* by *January 2022* as measured by *my daily walking log* .

      Insert Goal   Insert Date   Insert Measurement

Strategies to Accomplish the SMART Goal

Strategy 1. Schedule a daily designated time for walking with my wife.

Strategy 2. Start with 1 mile and gradually build up to 3 miles as my strength increases.

Strategy 3. Maintain a daily walking log to keep track of my progress.

SMART Goal Tracking Sheet for the HEALTH Domain

Factor	SMART Goal	Start Date	Complete Date

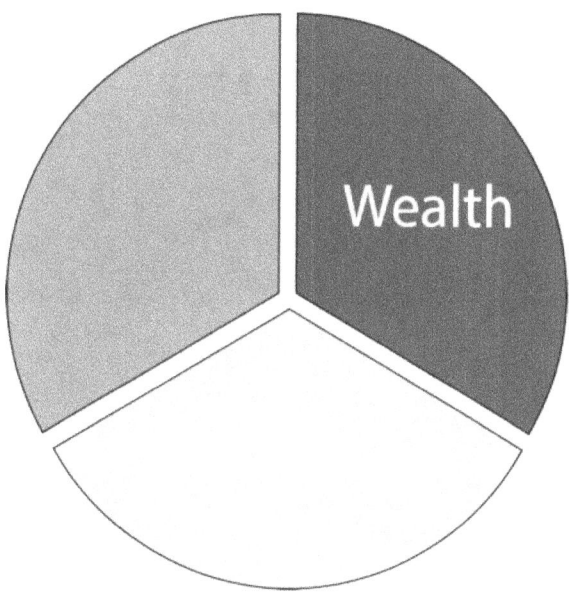

Wealth Domain

The Wealth Domain is concerned with how many sources and how much income the individual will have in retirement. It includes the six factors or Social Security, pensions, tax-deferred accounts, savings, investments, and work. The goal is to have as many income sources as possible and as much income as needed to maintain the worker's standard of living during the working years, as well as into and throughout retirement regardless of the number of years.

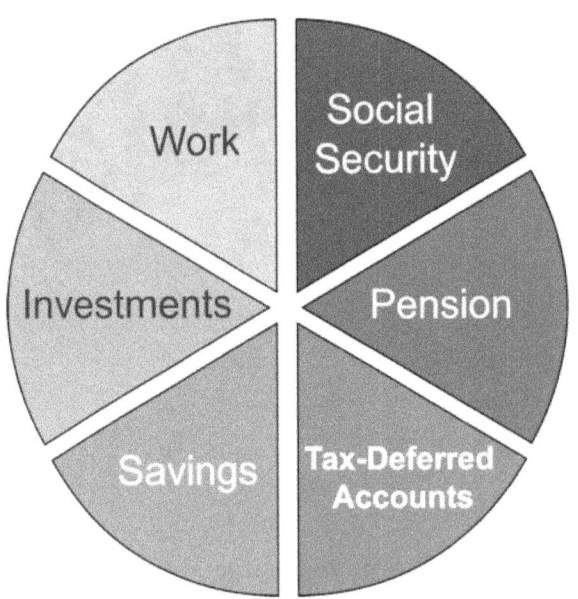

Wealth Factors

Chapter 7
SOCIAL SECURITY

*How do you know when it's time to retire? It's when you stop
lying about your age and start bragging about it.*
Unknown

The following summary of the Social Security factor which was first introduced in *Discover the Right Retirement for You*. The reader may choose to use this summary, or review the complete description in that book, to create and complete your short- and long-term retirement goals for the Social Security factor.

Social Security was designed to replace 40 percent of the average worker's pre-retirement income as a "social safety net." Workers preparing to retire often do a simple calculation of their current salary multiplied by 40 percent to estimate their anticipated Social Security benefits. This simple calculation is not only inaccurate but routinely results in an inflated benefits estimate, for a number of reasons. First, many of the workers have an income higher than the average worker, and Social Security benefits replace less than 40 percent the more an individual earns beyond the salary of the average worker. Second, Social Security benefits are calculated using a complicated formula termed the Average Indexed Monthly Earnings (AIME) based upon the worker's 35 highest earning years, adjusted for inflation, with lower earning years replaced by higher earning years and zeros averaged into the formula for any earning years that fall below the total of 35. The AIME is used to calculate the Primary Insurance Amount (PIA), which is the monthly Social Security benefit at the retiree's Full Retirement Age (FRA). Third, Social Security is not an unlimited benefits program, but rather it has a cap on all benefits, which helps support lower-wage earners at the expense of higher-wage earners. Fourth, this simple calculation produces a gross, not a net estimated amount, which fails to include a variety of deductions such as taxes, Medicare premiums, and garnishments. And lastly, many workers, especially those employed in public sector jobs, are not eligible for or receive reduced Social Security benefits because of a regulation termed the Government Pension Offset (GPO). This misinformation and these miscalculations have a significant negative impact on retirement planning by overestimating Social Security benefits, underestimating Medicare costs, and not estimating other deductions.

A retiree can start collecting Social Security benefits as early as age 62 and as late as age 70. The Full Retirement Age (FRA) has been increasing due to federal legislation passed in 1983. The FRA formerly was 65 for everyone. For those born in 1937 or earlier, the FRA remains age

65. For those born in 1960 or later, the FRA is 67. For those born between 1937 and 1960, the FRA is somewhere in between calculated on their birth month and year. Social Security benefits are decreased by about 30 percent if the worker files at age 62 instead of the FRA. Conversely, social security benefits increase by about 8 percent annually for every year beyond the FRA the worker delays collecting benefits until age 70 when they are capped for life. The worker can increase their Social Security benefits by 50 percent on average by delaying the filing for benefits from age 62 to age 70.

Social Security is designed to pay the retiree the same total lifetime benefit regardless of when they initially file. Filing earlier reduces the monthly benefits, but there are more payments. Filing later increases the monthly benefits, but there are fewer payments. This arrangement assumes the retiree will reach their average life expectancy, which currently is age 84.3 for men and age 86.7 for women. Retirees who surpass their average life expectancy benefit most from this arrangement. Occasionally, Social Security benefits are increased by a Cost of Living Adjustment (COLA), which was 1.6 percent in 2020 for a modest average monthly benefit payment increase of only $23. [12]

Social Security benefits are gender neutral, which means that workers with identical earnings are treated the same. Unfortunately, the workforce is gender biased, with women receiving Social Security benefits on average that are significantly lower than men because women frequently work part-time instead of full-time, are out of the workforce for extended periods of time for childbirth and parenting , and earn less than men for the same job. The gender pay gap, in which women earn about $.80 for every $1.00 men earn, has improved little during the last decade. The result is a lower AIME used to calculate a lower PIA for women than men. The historical view of the man as head of the household and breadwinner has also contributed to the maintenance of the gender pay gap and continued depression of Social Security benefits for women, even though they now are the primary breadwinner in 40 percent of all households. [13] Special attention should be paid to the pre-retirement estimation of Social Security benefits by women, since the gender pay gap is anticipated to continue indefinitely.

Social Security benefits are progressive, which means a higher-wage worker receives a higher total dollar benefit than a lower-wage worker, up to a current cap of $3,698 monthly. Since Social Security is designed to replace 40 percent of the pre-retirement income of the average-wage worker, that worker and the below-average-wage worker receive the 40 percent benefit, but a smaller dollar amount. In order for the above-average-wage worker to receive the maximum Social Security benefit, the worker would need to have the maximum taxable income for 35 years and delay receiving the benefit until age 70. Only 6 percent of all covered workers have earnings above the maximum Federal Insurance Contributions Act (FICA) taxable income of $137,700 in any given year and only 4 percent of Social Security recipients wait until age 70 to receive benefits. [14] As of December 2017, Social Security recipients received an average monthly benefit payment of $1,112 at age 62, $1,383 at age 66, and $1,510 at age 70, which is far below the current Social Security cap and barely above the national poverty level. [15] When Social Security benefits are aggregated, the average monthly benefit was $1,422 in 2018 and grew slightly to $1,461 in 2019.

Social Security benefits are not intended to be the only retirement income source, but rather the base upon which other retirement income sources are added. Without other income sources to supplement Social Security benefits, a retiree will not be able to achieve the 80 percent pre-retirement income level needed to maintain their standard of living in retirement. There is a big difference between the 40 percent Social Security guarantee for the average and below-average wage earners and the 80 percent standard of living target. There is a growing body of research that refutes the commonly held belief that costs will be significantly decreased in retirement since many retirees do not take the necessary actions to reduce spending, or if they do, find that they are unhappy with the result and return to their pre-retirement spending habits.

Social Security benefits are further diminished in a number of ways. First, federal income tax is paid by some individuals who have other substantial retirement income. Second, thirteen states tax Social Security benefits. Third, the Medicare Part B monthly premium ranging from $144.30 to $460.50 is automatically deducted from the Social Security monthly benefits. And lastly, if the recipient files for Social Security benefits at age 62 and continues to work, the benefits are reduced by $1 for every $2 earned over $18,240 yearly between age 62 and the FRA. If the recipient files for Social Security benefits at the FRA and continues to work, the benefits are reduced by $1 for every $3 earned over $48,600 yearly between the FRA and age 70. The result is a cap on both Social Security benefits and the potential earnings until age 70 at which time the earnings are no longer restricted. [16]

Many workers will never receive Social Security benefits. These workers are known as "never beneficiaries" and fall into four categories. First, many of them are infrequent workers who did not earn the prerequisite 40 lifetime work credits to qualify for benefits. Second, many of them are legal immigrants who arrived in the United States later in life and did not have enough time to earn the prerequisite 40 lifetime work credits to qualify for benefits. Third, many of them have qualified by earning the prerequisite 40 lifetime work credits, but will die before applying for benefits at age 62 or any time thereafter if they delayed applying for benefits after age 62, but before age 70. And lastly, many of them are employed in public sector jobs and are not eligible for benefits because of the Government Pension Offset (GPO). The Social Security Administration (SSA) benefits from "never beneficiaries" because they pay into the system, but receive no benefits.

Retirees interviewed for the book who were satisfied with the Social Security factor in their retirement reported that they had done the research to calculate a fairly accurate monthly benefit payment, but like so many other retirees had not calculated all of the possible deductions. A number of them had purposely delayed filing for Social Security benefits until after they had retired with the average being at their FRA. Less than 2 percent had waited until age 70 to file for Social Security benefits. It is noteworthy that most of them were quite knowledgeable about Social Security and had maximized their benefits to the extent possible using that knowledge. All of them described some form of benefits monitoring and management. And lastly, all of them complained about the size of their monthly benefit check, the small COLA, the lack of service by the Social Security Administration (SSA), and the fear that the system was going bankrupt.

Anthony is a good example of a retiree who is satisfied with the Social Security factor in his retirement. He retired at age 62, but did not apply for Social Security benefits until his FRA after he calculated that his monthly benefits check would be sufficient to help support his elderly parents who were living with him and his wife in a multigenerational household. He worked part-time between his FRA and age 70 and was careful to stay within the earning limit set by Social Security. It was evident that he monitored the monthly direct deposit of his benefits check and he stayed current with any changes to the program. Of particular interest was that Anthony was politically active when it came to federal legislation that could potentially impact him and his family. You will meet up with Anthony again in Chapter 14.

Retirees interviewed for the book who wanted a more rewarding retirement associated with their Social Security had done little, if any research to calculate their monthly benefit payment. An astonishing 50 percent reported that they just waited for their first check to see how much they would be receiving. Almost all of them had filed for Social Security benefits at age 62 and were equally divided between those who had to apply that early because of financial circumstances and those who chose to apply that early because they felt they deserved it after paying into the system for so long. It was noteworthy that most of them were uninformed about Social Security in general and did little to monitor and manage their benefits. Just like their counterparts noted above, all of them complained about the size of their monthly benefit check, the small COLA, the lack of service by the Social Security Administration (SSA), and the fear that the system was going bankrupt. The consistency between the retirees in both groups related to their complaints about Social Security was remarkable.

Nina is a good example of a retiree who wants a more rewarding retirement associated with her Social Security. She barely met the 40 lifetime work credits, with a number of gaps in employment as she frequently changed jobs, never really finding the right job for her. She filed for Social Security benefits at age 62 and was surprised to discover how small her monthly benefit check was, especially when she was told by her friends that she would receive 40 percent of her salary. Her monthly benefit check was further reduced when she reached age 65 and had to apply for Medicare. She was upset at the manner in which she was treated by the employees at the local Social Security office, but it appeared as if she was really upset about the bad news they shared with her related to the size of her benefits, and the like. Nina is in an unfavorable financial position, especially related to her minimal Social Security benefits, and is considering returning to the workforce.

In summary, retirees interviewed for the book who were satisfied with their retirement reported that they were able to monitor, manage, and maximize their Social Security benefits as represented by the following figure. The reader is encouraged to create a short- or long-term retirement goal in one or more of these areas, if determined to be appropriate after self-reflection, by taking the following steps.

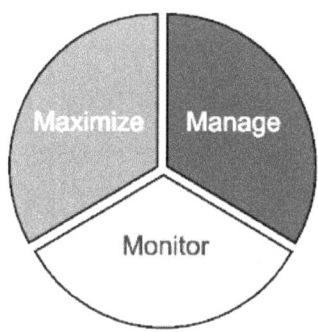

Suggested Topics for Creating a
Social Security Retirement Goal

- ☐ Review and reflect on the information contained in the chapter.

- ☐ Refer back to the detailed information about the Social Security factor contained in *Discover the Right Retirement for You* if you need to and have not already done so.

- ☐ Complete the SMART goal worksheet and compare *My Description of What is Now* with *My Description of What Will Be.*

- ☐ Create a short- or long-term SMART goal as appropriate.

- ☐ Select specific strategies to successfully accomplish the goal and implement them.

- ☐ Revisit the process as often as necessary, as you accomplish each goal or conditions change.

SMART Goal Worksheet

Domain: *Wealth*   Factor: *Social Security*

Directions: Complete *My Description of What Is Now* and *My Description of What Will Be*. If they match there is nothing to do. If they do not match create a short- or long-term SMART goal including specific strategies to accomplish the goal.

My Description of What Is Now	My Description of What Will Be

SMART Goal
Specific – Measurable – Achievable – Realistic – Timely

I will _____ by _____ as measured by _____.
      Insert Goal   *Insert Date*   *Insert Measurement*

Strategies to Accomplish the SMART Goal

Strategy 1. _____
Strategy 2. _____
Strategy 3. _____

Chapter 8
PENSION

Retire from work, not from life.
M. K. Soni

The following is a summary of the pension factor which was first introduced in *Discover the Right Retirement for You.* The reader may choose to use this summary, or review the complete description in that book, to create and complete your short- and long-term retirement goals for the pension factor.

Pension plans are not a new idea. Military pensions can be traced back to ancient Rome when soldiers were guaranteed income after they retired from active military service. This military benefit came to the United States when soldiers who survived the Civil War were rewarded with a lifetime income. Local, state, and federal governments have provided public sector pension plans for civil servants for many decades to offset lower pay during their working years with lifetime benefits during their retirement. The first private sector pension plan in the United States was created in 1875 by the American Express Company, and since that time they have been provided by virtually all large private companies and many smaller ones. Private sector pension plans have been a preference of private businesses for the recruitment and retention of highly skilled employees, much like that of public sector pension plans, but with different rules, regulations, and requirements.

There are two types of pension plans. The Defined Benefit Pension Plan is frequently referred to as a final salary or career average pension plan. Both the employee and the employer contribute to the pension plan during the employee's working years using a specified formula. The employer, or a representative of the employer, is responsible to invest the combined contributions to ensure there is enough money to pay the pension benefits at a specified amount in regular payments for the life of the retiree. If there is a shortfall, referred to as the net pension liability and defined as the difference between the pension fund assets and the amount of projected retiree payments, the employer must make up the deficit in order to guarantee the pension benefits. The employee's pension benefits are usually calculated using the following standard formula: final annual salary X benefit percent based upon age at retirement X total years of service = guaranteed pension benefit. The older the worker and the more years on the job, the greater the monthly retirement benefit payment. Many Defined Benefit Pension Plans include a Cost of Living Adjustment (COLA), which is an increase in retirement benefits paid either annually if a specified part of the pension plan, or periodically if investment returns exceed projections.

The Defined Contribution Pension Plan is frequently referred to as a money purchase or retirement savings pension plan. The contributions are guaranteed, since they are made by the employee and frequently matched by the employer up to certain thresholds. However, the final retirement income is not a guaranteed amount. The employee is responsible to invest the money in one of the employer's selected investment plans, and the pension benefits vary based upon the total contributions, the investment returns, and how the employee decides to withdraw their money from the pension fund during retirement. The more the employee contributes to the retirement fund, the greater the monthly retirement benefit payment, if the funds are wisely invested.

Tax-deferred or tax-sheltered accounts encourage the worker to save part of their income for retirement, receive matching company contributions in some instances, increase the pension fund, and reduce current taxes. Taxes are paid when the retiree withdraws the money, starting as early as age 59½ with required withdrawals, termed Required Minimum Distributions (RMD), starting at age 70½. The retiree can withdraw more than the RMD, but failure to make at least the required annual RMD results in a 50 percent IRS penalty, as well as any other federal tax that is due on the amount. These investment plans include 401(k) and 403(b) accounts, 457 Health Savings Accounts (HSA), and Individual Retirement Accounts (IRA). The SECURE Act passed on December 20, 2019, extended the age for first required RMD withdrawals to age 72. Defined Contribution Pension Plans usually do not have a Cost of Living Adjustment (COLA).

Regardless of the pension plan, the worker must be vested in order to eventually receive retirement benefits. In order to do this, the worker must meet the employer requirements as defined in the pension plan. The most common type of vesting requirement is the number of employment years on the job. For instance, a company may require the worker to be employed for five years before being vested in the pension plan. Once the worker completes the five years, the company includes the worker in the pension plan and gives the worker credit for the previous five years of work. If the worker leaves the company before the five years, there is no vesting. This is particularly important for a worker in a Defined Benefit Pension Plan, because the worker typically forfeits any of their contributions with no walk-away money if they leave the job before they are vested. Conversely, a worker in a Defined Contribution Pension Plan can withdraw their contributions and transfer them into some other investment vehicle without penalty if within a specified time and in accordance with state and federal laws. The vesting period varies by company.

Many local, state, and the federal governments still offer Defined Benefit Pension Plans at the urging, and many times at the insistence of powerful labor unions. However, there has been a dramatic shift in public sector pension plans since the early 1980s from Defined Benefit Pension Plans to Defined Contribution Pension Plans for a number of financial reasons. Public sector employers have experienced significant net pension liability due to escalating pension benefit costs and market volatility, which inhibit accurate long-term financial forecasting. At the same time, employees want to direct their own investments, with the anticipation of higher earnings than can be realized through employer investment vehicles. The investment risk is transferred from the employer to the employee. The employee has to decide how much investment risk can be tolerated financially and mentally. The bigger the investment risk, the bigger the potential financial returns and mental stress. This shift has reduced the number of workers participating in pension plans, especially those contributing to a Defined Contribution Pension Plan, because the worker's contribution and the amount of that contribution is voluntary. Their voluntary contributions seldom met the maximum allowed under law until well into their career when they are near retirement, leaving little time for catch-up contributions. [17]

The difference between a worker's anticipated and the retiree's actual pension plan retirement eligibility and benefits is cause for concern for a number of reasons. First, since so many workers are changing jobs so frequently, it is important to consider the type and quality of any pension plan. Second, coordinating pension plan participation from multiple jobs with an emphasis on vesting in each of them is important to maximize the final combined retirement benefits. Third, maximizing worker contributions in a Defined Contribution Pension Plan as early in a worker's career as possible is an effective retirement strategy for maximizing a pension fund through compound interest. And lastly, the bigger the pension plan fund balance, the less reliance on other sources of retirement income.

Retirees interviewed for the book who were satisfied with the pension factor in their retirement reported some obvious but important information. First, they actually had a pension plan, which had been secured over many years of work. Older retirees most often had a Defined Benefit Pension Plan and younger retirees most often had a Defined Contribution Pension Plan. Second, they knew what type of pension plan they had and could describe its features in detail. Third, they described the various ways in which they were able to maximize their pension. These ways included longevity in a single lifelong job, coordinating a number of pension plans from different jobs, working for a company with the best pension plan even if the salary was lower than expected, and long-term retirement planning focused on financial independence throughout their retirement no matter how long it lasted. They all spoke to the active monitoring and managing of their pension plans.

Stephanie is a good example of a retiree who is satisfied with her pension in retirement. She worked for a private company her entire career, but changed jobs within the company as promotional opportunities became available. She said that she had plenty of job offers from other companies, but always turned them down in order to remain where she was. When asked why she stayed with the company so long, she said that "They [her bosses] were real down-to-earth folks and treated me like family" and "I knew that I would be taken care of when I retired." She was able to clearly describe her retirement benefits from the Defined Benefit Pension Plan operated by the company and described her monthly pension check as "always arriving exactly on time every month." She even bragged a little bit about knowing exactly when her annual Cost of Living Adjustment (COLA) was due and that she made sure it was accounted for in her monthly check each year. It was evident that all of her pension planning had paid off for her in retirement.

Retirees interviewed for the book who wanted a more rewarding retirement associated with their pension initially treated pension planning and participation as an afterthought instead of an essential building block for financial security in retirement. They all knew that they would get a pension after they retired, but they did little if any research about its features and how it coordinated with other retirement income sources like Social Security. It was noteworthy that more than one-half of them said that they decided to retire without actually knowing what would be their pension income. One retiree summed it up by saying "I just thought that I would have plenty of money from my pension because I had worked for so many years. So I didn't worry much about it." The fantasy did not match the facts. The great majority of the retirees said that their pension benefits were far smaller than they had anticipated, which put a strain on their overall retirement income and budget. A frequent refrain from them was to lament their lack of pension planning with a typical "if I knew then what I know now" attitude.

Gregory is a good example of a retiree who wants a more rewarding retirement associated with his pension. He made an impressive amount of money during his career by chasing the money—that is, jumping from job to job as competing companies offered him ever-increasing salaries because of his talent in the high-tech field. He did not spend enough time in his early career at any one company to be vested, so the opportunity to coordinate his various pension plan benefits did not exist, because he had no pension plan rights. Regrettably, he did not vest and contribute to any of the Defined Contribution Pension Plans offered by the companies for which he worked until very late in his career, and then he did not make significant contributions to catch up, because he was so used to spending instead of saving. Immediate money was more important to him than long-term security. Gregory has now returned to the part-time workforce to supplement his retirement income and expects to do so for quite some time. This was not how he wanted to spend his retirement.

In summary, retirees interviewed for the book who were satisfied with their retirement reported that they were able to monitor, manage, and maximize their pension as represented by the following figure. The reader is encouraged to create a short- or long-term retirement goal in one or more of these areas, if determined to be appropriate after self-reflection, by taking the following steps.

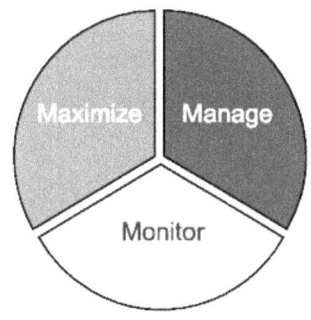

Suggested Topics for Creating a
Pension Retirement Goal

☐ Review and reflect on the information contained in the chapter.

☐ Refer back to the detailed information about the pension factor contained in *Discover the Right Retirement for You* if you need to and have not already done so.

☐ Complete the SMART goal worksheet and compare *My Description of What is Now* with *My Description of What Will Be*.

☐ Create a short- or long-term SMART goal as appropriate.

☐ Select specific strategies to successfully accomplish the goal and implement them.

☐ Revisit the process as often as necessary, as you accomplish each goal or conditions change.

SMART Goal Worksheet

Domain: *Wealth* Factor: *Pension*

Directions: Complete *My Description of What Is Now* and *My Description of What Will Be*. If they match there is nothing to do. If they do not match create a short- or long-term SMART goal including specific strategies to accomplish the goal.

My Description of What Is Now	My Description of What Will Be

SMART Goal
Specific – Measurable – Achievable – Realistic – Timely

I will _____ by _____ as measured by _____.
          Insert Goal   Insert Date   Insert Measurement

Strategies to Accomplish the SMART Goal

Strategy 1. _____
Strategy 2. _____
Strategy 3. _____

Chapter 9
TAX-DEFERRED ACCOUNTS

*The question isn't at what age I want to retire,
it's at what income.*
George Foreman

The following is a summary of the tax-deferred accounts factor, which was first introduced in *Discover the Right Retirement for You*. The reader may choose to use this summary, or review the complete description in that book, to create and complete your short- and long-term retirement goals for the tax-deferred accounts factor.

A tax-deferred retirement account, often referred to as tax-sheltered, is one into which pre-tax contributions are deposited and interest is earned until withdrawal of the funds at a later date, which is usually during retirement. Taxes on the contributions and interest are deferred until withdrawal of the funds. There are three general types of tax-deferred retirement accounts: 401(k) or 403(b) accounts, 457 Health Savings Accounts (HSA), and Individual Retirement Accounts (IRA). Within the IRA category are numerous variations from which to select. The worker can take advantage of the tax-deferred status of these retirement accounts as well as the earned compound interest. Compound interest is the interest earned on the initial investment and on the interest received from the investment. The earlier the investment, the longer for compound interest to accrue, so invest as early as possible, even if it is a relatively small amount. For example, if $100 is initially invested and it earns 5 percent interest annually, there will be $105 at the end of the first year. There will be $110.25 at the end of the second year because of the $5 interest on the initial $100 investment and the $.25 interest on the $5 interest. Even if no more money is added to the initial investment, in 10 years there will be $162 and in 25 years there will be $340. Even small amounts invested for long periods of time result in large amounts due to compound interest. The "Rule of 72" is an easy way to estimate how a tax-deferred investment will grow over time due to compound interest. Simply divide 72 by the interest rate to determine how long it will take the initial investment to double in value. For example, if the interest rate is 9 percent the investment will double in value every 8 years. [18]

A 401(k) account is a tax-deferred retirement plan sponsored by a private sector employer as part of a Defined Contribution Pension Plan. A 403(b) account is a tax-deferred retirement plan similar to a 401(k), but offered through IRS-exempted organizations, such as school districts, religious organizations, hospitals, governmental organizations, and educational institutions as part of a Defined Contribution Pension Plan. The voluntary contributions are automatically deducted from the worker's monthly paycheck before state and federal taxes are calculated, hence the designation as tax-deferred. The 2020 pre-tax contribution limit for both plans is $19,500 with a catch-up provision of $6,500 if the employee is age 50 or older. Both plans have a Required Minimal Distribution (RMD) at age 70, but funds can start to be withdrawn as early as age 59½ without penalty. Failure to make at least the annual RMD withdrawal results in a significant financial penalty of 50 percent, as well as any other tax that is due on the RMD. [19] The SECURE Act passed on December 20, 2019, extended the age for first required RMD withdrawals to age 72.

A 457 Health Savings Account (HSA) allows a worker to contribute pre-tax money and withdraw it tax-free when spent on health insurance deductibles and other qualified medical expenses, including those for medical, dental and vision services. The annual 457 HSA contribution limit is $3,550 for individuals covered under a qualifying medical insurance plan and $7,100 for those covered under a qualifying family medical insurance plan. If the worker is age 55 or older they can contribute an additional $1,000 annually. Once the worker is eligible for Medicare they can make withdrawals, but cannot continue making tax-deferred contributions even if they are working. There is a 20 percent penalty plus other income tax due if the worker is under age 65 and withdraws money for any reason other than insurance deductibles and other qualified medical expenses. [20]

An Individual Retirement Account (IRA) is a personal, tax-deferred account created by the Internal Revenue Service (IRS) to give workers an easy way to save for retirement. There are seven types of IRAs: traditional IRA, Roth IRA, SEP IRA, nondeductible IRA, spousal IRA, SIMPLE IRA, and self-directed IRA. The traditional IRA uses pre-tax contributions to increase the fund until they are withdrawn and taxed as early as age 59½, but no later than age 72. The Roth IRA uses after-tax contributions to increase the fund until they are withdrawn without being taxed at any age. The Simplified Employee Pension (SEP) IRA has the same requirements as a traditional IRA, except the employer must make contributions as well as the employee. The nondeductible IRA uses taxed contributions like a Roth IRA, but only the interest and not the principle, is taxed upon withdrawal as early as age 59½, but no later than age 72. The spousal IRA has the same requirements as a traditional IRA, but is available to the spouse of a worker if the spouse is not working or has a minimal income. The Savings Incentive Match Plan for Employees (SIMPLE) IRA has the same requirements as a traditional IRA, but is offered through a small business employer. The self-directed IRA has the same requirements as a traditional IRA, but instead of having a common investment vehicle the worker owns assets directly. Since there are so many types of IRAs, each with its own requirements and contribution limits, it is important to understand the benefits and burdens of each type and make the decision of which one to select with the guidance of a financial advisor. [21]

There are many advantages to investing in a tax-deferred retirement account. The availability of such an account encourages the worker to save part of their income for retirement, receive matching company contributions in some instances, increase the pension fund, benefit from compound interest, and reduce current taxes. The tax will be deferred until such time as it is withdrawn, which is usually during retirement. A common misconception is that the retiree will be in a lower tax bracket at the time such withdrawals begin. This may not always be true. The tax bracket for many retirees does not change much, if at all, because of increased income sources and decreased tax deductions in retirement. There are a number of increased income sources in retirement. First, one in every six Americans receives Social Security benefits, and these are taxed in thirteen states—and under some conditions, by the federal government. Second, the tax deferral is eliminated, and taxes are paid once the annual RMD withdrawals begin. Third, pension plan benefits replace pre-retirement salary to varying amounts. The smaller the difference between the pre-retirement salary and post-retirement pension benefits, the larger the tax liability. And lastly, more retirees than ever before are returning to part-time and seasonal work to supplement their retirement income. Taxes are due on this income, no matter how small it may be. All of these factors increase retirement income and result in a greater tax liability. There are also a number of decreased tax deductions in retirement. First, tax deductions for dependents probably ceased many years earlier than retirement depending on the age of the retiree. Second, the house mortgage may be paid off, so there is no mortgage interest deduction. Third, retirees typically reduce their charitable contributions because they have less income, and replace them with volunteer work, since they have the time to do so. Fourth, work-related deductions, such as a home office, are eliminated as the retiree stops work. The home office is still there, but the work done in it is gone. And lastly, the deduction for tax-deferred retirement account contributions is eliminated and replaced by RMD taxable withdrawals. All of these factors decrease deductions and result in a greater tax liability. The combination of an increased income stream and decreased tax deductions may result in no change to the retiree's tax bracket.

Retirees interviewed for the book who were satisfied with the tax-deferred accounts in their retirement had taken advantage of such accounts early in their career and maintained a consistent contribution history until their retirement. The most popular tax-deferred accounts were the 401(k) and 403(b) accounts, followed closely by a variety of IRAs. When asked to explain this pattern, most of the retirees said that the 401(k) and 403(b) accounts were the easiest to access through their job and that the variety of IRAs were more confusing to them as an investment vehicle. There was universal agreement that these tax-deferred contributions were beneficial when undertaken in a consistent long-term manner. The myth of the lower tax bracket in retirement was laid bare by the accounts of most of the retirees interviewed, who reported that their tax bracket had not changed at all in retirement. Recent articles related to this phenomenon are beginning to question the advisability of such tax-deferred contributions in lieu of other investment vehicles. The preference still remains an individual one.

Hugh is a good example of a retiree who is satisfied with the tax-deferred accounts factor in his retirement. He was diligent in contributions to his 403(b) account offered by the school district in which he worked as a teacher. His contributions increased proportionately as he received annual raises, no matter what the amount. He did not participate in any IRAs and when asked about this he said that he found them "too confusing and it was easier to invest in the 403(b) plan offered right where I worked." Hugh is taking the RMD from his 403(b) account and is satisfied with the investment and its monthly benefit payment. As with so many other retirees, Hugh was surprised that he did not change his tax bracket once he retired, because that was what he had always been told by others. It is just one of the many myths about retirement that has little basis in reality.

Retirees interviewed for the book who wanted a more rewarding retirement associated with their tax-deferred accounts told a very different story. Most of them invested little, or nothing at all, in either a tax-sheltered account or an IRA. When asked about this lack of pre-retirement investment, their most common response was that they did not have the money to do so, given the financial demands of raising a family, and the like. Very few of them had more than a fundamental understanding of the power of long-term investment, compound interest, and deferred taxes, which are the fundamentals of these retirement investment options. As part of the interview process, they were presented with a simple financial example of a typical 401(k) investment and its cumulative result over a 40 year work career. They were amazed at what could have been and dismayed about what they had now. Their opportunity to even consider participation now was gone because they were already retired and no longer working.

Ted is a good example of a retiree who wants a more rewarding retirement associated with his tax-deferred account. He invested early and consistently into a 401(k) tax-deferred account throughout his working career because he knew the retirement benefit that he would ultimately receive. This is a good thing. However, raising a family of three sons took lots of money, and his contributions were very modest in relation to what he could have contributed. His final monthly benefit payments are equally modest in retirement. This is not so good. Ted had the right idea and if he had been more aggressive in his contributions he would be in a better financial situation in his retirement. When presented with the 401(k) investment example identified in the previous paragraph and extrapolated with a larger amount that Ted could have invested, he was surprised at the significant amount that he could have had in retirement. Ted is an unfortunate example of "too little, too late."

In summary, retirees interviewed for the book who were satisfied with their retirement reported that they were able to monitor, manage, and maximize their tax-deferred accounts as represented by the following figure. The reader is encouraged to create a short- or long-term retirement goal in one or more of these areas, if determined to be appropriate after self-reflection, by taking the following steps.

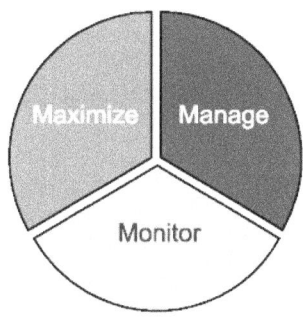

Suggested Topics for Creating a
Tax-Deferred Accounts Retirement Goal

☐ Review and reflect on the information contained in the chapter.

☐ Refer back to the detailed information about the tax-deferred accounts factor contained in *Discover the Right Retirement for You* if you need to and have not already done so.

☐ Complete the SMART goal worksheet and compare *My Description of What is Now* with *My Description of What Will Be.*

☐ Create a short- or long-term SMART goal as appropriate.

☐ Select specific strategies to successfully accomplish the goal and implement them.

☐ Revisit the process as often as necessary, as you accomplish each goal or conditions change.

SMART Goal Worksheet

Domain: *Wealth*   Factor: *Tax-Deferred Accounts*

Directions: Complete *My Description of What Is Now* and *My Description of What Will Be*. If they match there is nothing to do. If they do not match create a short- or long-term SMART goal including specific strategies to accomplish the goal.

My Description of What Is Now	My Description of What Will Be

SMART Goal
Specific – Measurable – Achievable – Realistic – Timely

I will _____ by _____ as measured by _____.
         Insert Goal   Insert Date   Insert Measurement

Strategies to Accomplish the SMART Goal

Strategy 1. _____
Strategy 2. _____
Strategy 3. _____

Chapter 10
SAVINGS

For many people being asked to solve their own retirement savings problems is like being asked to build their own car.
Richard Thaler

The following is a summary of the savings factor, which was first introduced in *Discover the Right Retirement for You*. The reader may choose to use this summary, or review the complete description in that book, to create and complete your short- and long-term retirement goals for the savings factor.

From the time we are young children, our parents encourage us to save because nothing is free and everything comes at a cost. This has come to be called the piggy bank mentality, and it originated during the Middle Ages when people saved coins in orange-colored clay pots made of pygg. As the spoken word became less associated with the orange-colored clay pygg pot and more with the animal, it was only a matter of time before someone fashioned a pygg pot in the shape of a real pig. Hence the reason why there are no elephant banks, lion banks, and the like. The transition from pig to piggy soon followed because of the popularity of the pygg pot with children, as did the transition from pot to bank, which was the original intended use of the pot. Earlier versions of the pygg pot did not have a hole in the bottom and had to be smashed to retrieve the valuable contents. The message was about the seriousness of saving, the difficulty in accessing the accumulated money, and the importance of making a wise spending decision. The modern day piggy bank has a hole in the bottom closed with a plug in order to remove the savings without damaging the bank. The message remains the same about the seriousness of saving, but it is easy to access the accumulated money while recycling the bank for future savings.

It is important to calculate how much money a retiree will need from all income sources, including savings, during their retirement. Many retirees forget to factor in the effects of inflation, which is the numeric value of the rate at which the price of goods and services increases over time. Put in a different way, inflation is the decrease of purchasing power and the increase in the money the retiree will need to purchase the same goods and services from year to year. Most experts recommend using a 3 percent yearly inflation rate when calculating any budget. For example, if the retiree calculates they will need $12,000 from their savings the first year of retirement, they will need $12,360 from their savings the next year of retirement for the same goods and services. Do not underestimate the erosion of purchasing power due to the negative effects of inflation.

A savings account is an account in a bank or other financial institution, such as a credit union, in which you store your money safely while earning interest. A savings account is the safest way to invest your money with minimal risk and the easiest way to retrieve your money quickly. It is insured by the Federal Deposit Insurance Company (FDIC), which is an independent federal agency with the responsibility to maintain public confidence in the United States banking system by insuring deposits in our banks in the event of a bank closure. An individual savings account is insured up to $250,000 under the FDIC protection. Multiple savings accounts are insured separately up to $250,000 even if they are all in the same bank or other financial institution. [22] In addition to a traditional savings account, there are other low-risk, interest-earning accounts into which savings can be invested. These include a checking account, certificate of deposit, treasury note, and municipal bonds. Savings bonds are also a form of savings investment in the United States government, which are purchased at face value and redeemed for full value at 30 years. [23] Regardless of which type of savings option in which your money is invested, it is important to do the research to decide which accounts yield the best interest and provide the level of financial security with which the investor is most comfortable. The smaller the risk, the smaller the potential financial gain and the lower the investment stress. The bigger the risk, the bigger the potential financial gain and the higher the investment stress.

Most workers describe their savings habits as the piggy bank mentality they inherited from their parents. Their main purpose for having a savings account is as a rainy day fund in case of an unforeseen emergency, such as car repair, a new kitchen appliance, and the like. The national trend is that 39 percent of workers have $0 savings and 18 percent of workers have less than $1,000 savings. [24] Most retirees do not consider a savings account an important part of their retirement plan because of the relatively small amount of funds in their account while they are working, which they bring into retirement. Many retirees actually reduce their already small savings account because of the elimination of the need for unexpected living expenses since "you cannot get fired from retirement." This narrow vision of savings in retirement does not provide the retiree with the flexibility to protect other retirement income sources, such as stocks and bonds, or to leverage other investment opportunities, such as starting a small business. It should be noted that a general increase in retiree bankruptcies is partially a result of the savings and credit card debt imbalance.

A closer examination of credit card debt is warranted because of the enormity of the problem existing before retirement which the worker then carries into retirement. Slightly more than 70 percent of all households have at least one credit card, and many households have multiple credit cards. About 25 percent of all households with a credit card have more credit card debt than savings. Whereas the average household has more than $15,000 in credit card debt, they have less than $1,000 in a savings account. This imbalance in a high credit card debt and low savings account balance should be of concern, since they are paying high interest on a big credit card debt while receiving low interest on a small savings account balance. The problem is compounded by maxing out the credit card while paying the minimum monthly payment. The minimum monthly credit card payment is usually one percent of the credit card balance plus interest. If this is all a credit card holder can regularly pay against their credit card debt, they are in serious financial trouble. Most financial planners recommend a credit card utilization rate of 30 percent or below. That means that a credit card holder uses only 30 percent of the total credit card limit available, leaving room on the credit card for unexpected short-term expenses which should be paid off as soon as possible. About 50 percent of all credit card purchases are discretionary and unnecessary. Flipping the balance to a low or no credit card debt and a high savings account fund balance is the first step in hitting the 50/30/20 budget target of 50 percent for essentials, 30 for discretionary spending, and 20 percent for savings.

There are two ways to increase a savings account balance: reduce expenses or create new income. Reducing and finally eliminating unnecessary discretionary purchases and paying down and finally eliminating credit card debt are the two keys to reducing expenses. A simple need versus want test will result in the reduction of certain expenses. A need is something that you must have to survive. A want is something that you would like to have, but is not needed to survive. When faced with a purchase, decide if it is a need, such as food, or a want, such as a pair of designer shoes. Spend on what you need, not what you want. The less that is spent today, the easier it is tomorrow to maintain your lifestyle in retirement. Replace the satisfaction of spending to obtain a thing with the satisfaction of saving to obtain financial peace of mind. [25] Most retirees will find it difficult to create new income. Paying yourself first with a modest monthly deposit into your savings account is the key to creating new income. Small savings result in large savings when the money is subjected to compound interest over time.

Retirees interviewed for the book who were satisfied with the savings in their retirement all had something in common. They all had a savings account and there was a significant fund balance in it. This may sound like an obvious statement, but it is noteworthy that 39 percent of workers have $0 savings and 18 percent of workers have less than $1,000 savings which they bring into retirement. Their savings account balances were far greater than $1,000 on average. All of the retirees said that they have tried to keep their credit card balances under control, with varying degrees of success, but in general they all reported credit card balances which they perceived to be acceptable as compared to their total retirement income. As part of the extended interview, they were asked if they decided on purchases using the need versus want approach, or some version thereof. The great majority clearly responded that a need always came before a want.

Manuel is a good example of a retiree who is satisfied with his savings in retirement. He said that he always had a rainy day savings account while he was working and brought it into his retirement. At the time of the interview, he had about $3,500 in the savings account and felt it was sufficient to cover any unforeseen emergency. It was noteworthy that his retirement budget included an automatic monthly payment of $150 to his savings account in order to increase the fund balance. He was very firm in his belief about credit cards as exemplified by the statement "I have one credit card and only one credit card. I do not understand how folks can have so many credit cards when they only need one. I pay the balance due at the end of the month whenever possible and only carry over a balance if something unexpected has happened. I still like using paper money whenever I can. Cash is king."

Retirees interviewed for the book who wanted a more rewarding retirement associated with their savings also had something in common. Most of them did not have a savings account, and if they did, the fund balance was very small. In most cases, it was well below $500. Their reliance on credit cards was amazing with many of them having five or more of them. When asked about this number of credit cards, their collective responses all seemed to try to defend the high number of credit cards with the following reasoning. "I only have one major credit card [like VISA, Mastercard, etc.] and the remaining ones are smaller [they had smaller approved spending limits]." It appeared as if they thought they had two types of credit cards, the major one and all the others. Regardless of this type of reasoning, a credit card is still a credit card, and caution must be taken with credit card balances that can easily get away from the retiree, especially with multiple credit cards. As part of the extended interview, they were asked if they decided on purchases using the need versus want approach, or some version thereof. Their responses were almost equal between need and want purchases.

Cassandra is a good example of a retiree who wants a more rewarding retirement associated with her savings. She did have a savings account, but the fund balance was so low that the bank was charging her a monthly service fee just to keep the savings account open. She was literally paying the bank to keep her money, and the monthly fee was larger than the monthly interest she received from the bank. By increasing the fund balance by only $100, that monthly service fee would disappear, but she had not made that deposit. It was almost as if she felt secure that she had a saving account even though the fund balance was so small. She compounded this situation by having 11 different credit cards, all for different reasons she was able to explain and that she was happy to show the interviewer. She reported that all of the credit cards had some balance due on them, but she paid something toward each credit card monthly. Again, it was as if she felt secure that she made a payment on each of the credit cards monthly, not realizing that she was slowly going deeper into debt because of the credit card balance carried over monthly. Her self-proclaimed hobby was going shopping for shoes, which was clearly a confirmation of her discretionary want spending. Cassandra would be a prime candidate for financial counseling focused on budget management in her retirement.

In summary, retirees interviewed for the book who were satisfied with their retirement reported that they had decreased discretionary spending and credit card debt, as well as explored other income sources, as represented by the following figure. The reader is encouraged to create a short- or long-term retirement goal in one or more of these areas, if determined to be appropriate after self-reflection, by taking the following steps.

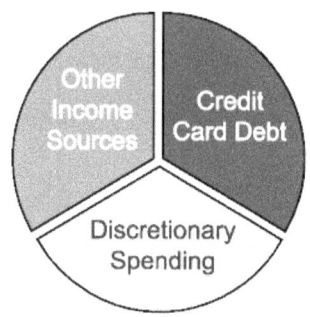

Suggested Topics for Creating a
Savings Retirement Goal

☐ Review and reflect on the information contained in the chapter.

☐ Refer back to the detailed information about the savings factor contained in *Discover the Right Retirement for You* if you need to and have not already done so.

☐ Complete the SMART goal worksheet and compare *My Description of What is Now* with *My Description of What Will Be.*

☐ Create a short- or long-term SMART goal as appropriate.

☐ Select specific strategies to successfully accomplish the goal and implement them.

☐ Revisit the process as often as necessary, as you accomplish each goal or conditions change.

SMART Goal Worksheet

Domain: *Wealth* **Factor:** *Savings*

Directions: Complete *My Description of What Is Now* and *My Description of What Will Be*. If they match there is nothing to do. If they do not match create a short- or long-term SMART goal including specific strategies to accomplish the goal.

My Description of What Is Now	My Description of What Will Be

SMART Goal
Specific – Measurable – Achievable – Realistic – Timely

I will _____ by _____ as measured by _____.
      Insert Goal   Insert Date   Insert Measurement

Strategies to Accomplish the SMART Goal

Strategy 1. _____
Strategy 2. _____
Strategy 3. _____

Chapter 11
INVESTMENTS

*Our seniors' retirement should never rely on the bull of
political promises or the bear of the market.*
Barbara Mikulski

The following is a summary of the investments factor, which was first introduced in *Discover the Right Retirement for You.* The reader may choose to use this summary, or review the complete description in that book, to create and complete your short- and long-term retirement goals for the investments factor.

Funds should be allocated to a variety of forms of investments in order to diversify your financial portfolio and not put the proverbial "all your eggs in one basket." Diversification is the spreading of investments, which react differently to the same economic event, to balance risk and yield a consistent combined return over time. There are six types of financial diversification. Industry diversification is the spreading of investments among a number of different types of industries. For example, the investor may put some of their money into technology, pharmaceutical research, and real estate. Company diversification is the spreading of investments among a number of different companies within the same industry. For example, the investor may put some money into McDonald's, Burger King, and Wendy's because they are all in the fast food business. Strategy diversification is the spreading of investments among low-risk, medium-risk, and high-risk ventures. For example, the investor may put some money into an established housing project with low risk and smaller returns, as well as some money into a new housing project with high risk and potential larger returns. Time diversification is the spreading of smaller investment amounts over time, termed dollar cost averaging, versus a larger lump sum investment amount at one time. For example, the investor may put $1,000 each year for five years into the New Valley Technology Company or the entire $5,000 into the company in one year. Geographic diversification is the spreading of investments internationally to avoid home country bias in which assets are only invested by someone in their own country. For example, the investor may put some money into an American-based company as well as into an Indian-based company. And lastly, asset class diversification is the spreading of available assets among a number of options previously described. [26]

Many retirees report that they have not invested in stocks or bonds because they have little understanding of the stock and bond markets and had such small amounts with which to invest. Stocks are an equity investment that represents shared ownership in a company and entitles the investor to part of the company's assets and earnings. There are both common and preferred stocks. An alternative to, or in addition to stocks, an investment can be made in bonds. A bond is a debt security similar to an IOU with interest. Borrowers issue bonds to raise money from investors willing to lend them money for a certain amount of time in return for the full loan repayment and interest. There are several types of bonds, including treasury bonds, agency bonds, corporate bonds, high-yield bonds, foreign bonds, mortgage-backed bonds, and municipal bonds. There are number of steps to take when investing in either stocks or bonds. First, do some research to understand how they work. Second, decide on an investment strategy and stick to it. Third, select the type of stocks or bonds in which you want to invest. Fourth, choose an investment horizon. Fifth, research the options before purchasing a certain stock or bond. Sixth, use a laddered approach to investment, in which stocks or bonds are purchased at staggered intervals in order to take advantage of changing interest rates at both the time of purchase and sale. [27] And lastly, it is always wise to work with a financial advisor in whom you have confidence for advice and guidance.

The term "the American dream" was coined by historian and author James Truslow Adams in 1931. He described it as "… that dream of a land in which life should be better and richer and fuller for everyone, with opportunity for each according to ability and achievement." [28] The most frequently cited example of "the American dream" is home ownership because it is a symbol of financial success by being able to afford a house, and independence by being able to do whatever the owner wants to the house. Buying a house is the biggest single investment made by most people as part of their investments.

There are advantages and disadvantages to home ownership. Home ownership completes "the American dream" and creates pride in that ownership while providing a return on investment (ROI). The homeowner can make substantial changes to the property, such as custom paint, structural changes, and the like. A single-family detached home usually has more privacy than a rental unit in a complex. Conversely, home ownership requires maintenance and upkeep. Owning a home with a mortgage drives up the debt-to-income ratio, putting a strain on your credit. Home ownership limits your current job and future retirement mobility. Many retirees find it difficult to sell the big house they bought during their working years and downsize, especially in desirable retirement locations, because most other homeowners are doing the same thing. There are just too many of these too-big homes. [29]

There are advantages to renting. Rent payments are usually lower than mortgage payments with lower up-front and move-in costs. Utility costs are usually included in the rent payment. The monthly rent payment is predictable, and there is usually advance notice of a rent increase. The rental agency is responsible for repairs and upkeep. The renter can easily relocate for a job promotion or other opportunity. There are also disadvantages to renting. There is no pride of ownership because the rental unit belongs to someone else. The renter does not get a return on investment (ROI) because you are making someone else's mortgage payment. The renter cannot make substantial changes to the property. Renters lose some amount of privacy, with many rental units in close proximity to one another, and common areas shared by all of them.

Retirees interviewed for the book were satisfied with the investments in their retirement. These included some stocks and bonds, as well as a variety of other small low-cost investments. Many of them owned their home, which was usually mortgage-free. Since almost all of them were, or had been homeowners, and this was their single most expensive investment, most of the interview was directed toward questions about this investment. The prevailing feeling for those retirees who still owned their home was that it was a lifelong investment that they were saving to pass on to their children as part of their estate. This was commendable, but their money was tied up in the home and was not creating any form of retirement income. Those retirees who viewed their home as a tangible investment had either sold their home as part of the transition to retirement or were thinking about doing so in the near future. The prevailing feeling for those retirees was that it was a lifelong investment to be turned into cash as a retirement income source. Their retirement living arrangements included renting an apartment, living with family members in a multigenerational home, assistive living facilities, and a few other options. Even these retirees spoke about having some money left when they died to pass on to their children as part of their estate. Both groups of retirees had a commendable goal to leave some money in their estate for their children, but had approached it in very different ways.

Jean is a good example of a retiree who is satisfied with her investments in retirement. She had lived in the same small house with her husband and children until she retired following the unexpected passing of her husband. She sold the mortgage-free home and began using the money as part of her retirement income. Her children were insistent that she live with one of them and she moved in with her eldest son and his family in a house close to the old neighborhood. She spoke volumes about how happy she was with this arrangement and her contribution to the family by doing some cooking and other activities around the house. She was particularly outspoken about being with her family and the enjoyment she received when she spent time with her grandchildren. Instead of keeping all of her money in a savings account, she took the advice of her eldest son and invested some of it in a 10-year certificate of deposit. When asked why she selected the 10-year option, she said "I expect to still be around for the next 10 years and will decide what to do with it at that time." She gives all of her children a small monthly amount with the admonishment that "I would sooner give it to them now when they need it for themselves and their families instead of leaving to them when I die."

Retirees interviewed for the book who wanted a more rewarding retirement associated with investments frequently reported no investments whatsoever, including that of a house. The most common reason for not owning a home was the cost. It is important to note that owning a home is a costly endeavor and one which requires some significant monetary sacrifices, for most people. For some people, owning a home is simply not within their financial ability. There were two important questions asked during the interviews in order to shed some light on this situation.

First, the retirees were asked what they had done for a living. They consistently reported jobs that were described as blue collar, but not requiring any formal training like an apprenticeship to become a plumber, electrician, and the like. Most reported jobs in the hospitality and retail economic sectors. Second, the retirees were asked about their annual salary. They consistently reported annual salaries near or at the poverty level. These retirees painted a picture of economic poverty which never improved for them. They had longevity on the job, but no elevation in income. Their "American dream" was unfulfilled.

Lawrence is a good example of a retiree who wants a more rewarding retirement associated with investments. He worked in the fast food industry for his entire life and said that "I jumped from job to job because that's the nature of the business." His modest income did not allow him to save very much, since he was barely able to pay for the essentials. Lawrence always had to have one or more roommates in order to pay the rent, so the idea of owning a home was out of the question. He recounted a life on the edge of financial insecurity. Retirement has not been much better for him, since he is still renting, but now on an even more limited income. When asked what he would have done differently if given the opportunity to do so, he responded "I wish I had tried harder to get better jobs and improve myself, but the time just slipped away. So here I am no better off than when I started working 40 years ago."

In summary, retirees interviewed for the book who were satisfied with their retirement reported that they were able to monitor, manage, and maximize their investments, including a house, as represented by the following figure. The reader is encouraged to create a short- or long-term retirement goal in one or more of these areas, if determined to be appropriate after self-reflection, by taking the following steps.

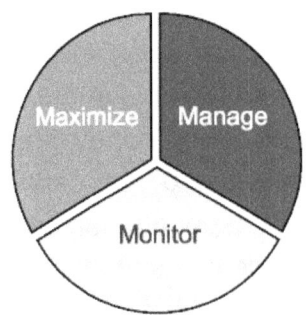

Suggested Topics for Creating an
Investments Retirement Goal

- ☐ Review and reflect on the information contained in the chapter.

- ☐ Refer back to the detailed information about the investments factor contained in *Discover the Right Retirement for You* if you need to and have not already done so.

☐ Complete the SMART goal worksheet and compare *My Description of What is Now* with *My Description of What Will Be.*

☐ Create a short- or long-term SMART goal as appropriate.

☐ Select specific strategies to successfully accomplish the goal and implement them.

☐ Revisit the process as often as necessary, as you accomplish each goal or conditions change.

SMART Goal Worksheet

Domain: *Wealth* Factor: *Investments*

Directions: Complete *My Description of What Is Now* and *My Description of What Will Be*. If they match there is nothing to do. If they do not match create a short- or long-term SMART goal including specific strategies to accomplish the goal.

My Description of What Is Now	My Description of What Will Be

SMART Goal
Specific – Measurable – Achievable – Realistic – Timely

I will _____ by _____ as measured by _____.
           Insert Goal   Insert Date   Insert Measurement

Strategies to Accomplish the SMART Goal

Strategy 1. _____
Strategy 2. _____
Strategy 3. _____

Chapter 12
WORK

Whether you are just entering the workforce or nearing retirement age, planning for the future is critical.
Ron Lewis

The following is a summary of the work factor, which was first introduced in *Discover the Right Retirement for You.* The reader may choose to use this summary, or review the complete description in that book, to create and complete your short- and long-term retirement goals for the work factor.

From the time we are young students in school, we are asked "What do you want to be when you grow up?" We are not asked what kind of person we want to be, but rather what we want to be. The former is about character, the latter is about career. The distinction is important. There have been a multitude of articles written about not letting your career, and especially a certain job, define you. All that goes away once you are retired. Or does it? Baby Boomers in increasing numbers are experiencing a variety of different retirement options and are deciding to not retire, or at least delay it, for a number of reasons. These reasons include financial problems, underfunding of pension plans, economic uncertainty, caring for elderly parents, and other problems specific to the retiree. It is important to explore each of these retirement options in order to select the best one for you, given your personality and view of work.

The first option is retirement with no work. Workers who anticipate not working after retirement typically view it as the destination at the end of a long journey. Their common refrain is "I am entitled to do nothing after working so many years," or some version thereof. They have a balance between their personal life and work and can tolerate an abrupt stop to their daily work routine without much stress. They have made plans to retire at a certain time but have not planned what to do after they retire.

The second option is a phased-in retirement with phased-out work. Workers who anticipate not working in retirement by phasing out work also typically view it as the destination at the end of a long journey, but are more cautious about the transition and want to try things out. Their common refrain is "I am eventually going to retire, but want to ease into it," or some version thereof. They have a balance between their personal life and work and can tolerate a gradual change and final termination to their daily routine without much stress if done in small steps. They have made plans to retire at a certain time, which may slightly change as they experience the gradual phasing-in of retirement and phasing-out of work.

The third option is retirement with continued part-time work. Workers who anticipate working part-time after retirement view it as the next phase in a lifelong journey. Their common refrain is "I want to keep active and connected in retirement," or some version thereof. They have a balance between their personal life and work and can tolerate some change, but no final termination of work. The complete termination of work is a source of great stress for them.

The fourth option is no retirement with continued full-time work. Workers who anticipate continuing to work full-time typically view work as an important part of their lifelong journey. Their common refrain is "I cannot see myself ever retiring," or some version thereof. It would be easy to brand these workers as addicted workaholics, but that is usually not the case. There are five types of people who will never retire: the worker who is forced to continue working due to financial problems; the successful investor who manipulates various markets to make money and does not see this activity as actual work; the life reinventor who still wants to try a lot of different things including other careers, often referred to as encore careers; the mega-successful lifer who is successful in whatever endeavor is undertaken; and the true workaholic who enjoys work and does it with enthusiasm. Any reduction or termination of work is a source of serious stress to them. [30]

Many times it takes money to make money. Be aware of the hidden costs of working during retirement, especially working part-time. First, getting to and from work will require either public or private transportation. Calculate the cost of public transportation if it is available and if the schedule fits your work hours. Then calculate the cost of private transportation, including the purchase of a car, insurance, gas, regular maintenance, and unexpected repairs. Many couples have two cars during their working years and then eliminate one of the cars as a cost-saving measure in retirement. Think about the impact this will have on your spouse if you are still using the remaining car to get to and from work. What does your spouse do for transportation when you are using the only car?

Second, expect to spend the same amount of daily commute time as when you were working. You may not notice any change if you continue to work full-time, but there will be a significant impact if you work part-time and still have an average one-hour commute each day.

Third, calculate incidental costs, especially lunch. For example, if you are working two hours each day at $12 per hour for a total of $24 per day and you spend $10 each day on lunch, your daily income is only $14 before taxes. Even bringing your lunch from home will still cost something.

Fourth, if you file for Social Security benefits at age 62 and continue to work, benefits will be reduced by $1 for every $2 earned over $18,240 yearly between age 62 and the FRA. If you file for Social Security benefits at the FRA and continue to work, the benefits will be reduced by $1 for every $3 earned over $48,600 yearly between the FRA and age 70. This has a significant negative effect on the worker who chooses to continue working full-time between ages 62 and 70. Consider deferring Social Security benefits until age 70 to maximize the benefits and eliminate the salary cap for full-time work. Try to stay under the Social Security earning caps for part-time work.

And lastly, time is money. Decide if this is how you want to spend part or all of your retirement days and whether it is worthwhile to do so financially. Many retirees try part-time work during retirement and find that their take-home salary is far less than they expected. When other factors are calculated, such as transportation, they are actually losing money on the deal. Think about doing volunteer work if this is the situation in which you find yourself.

Retirees interviewed for the book who were satisfied with the work factor in their retirement represented a diverse group of people. Approximately one-half of the retirees had fully retired with no work, while the remaining one-half of the retirees were still working. Of this group, almost all of them were working part-time, with less than five percent working full-time. The retirees who had fully retired with no work reported that they viewed it as the destination at the end of a long journey. When asked what they did in retirement, Charles summed it up for many of them when he said "Oh, I find plenty of things to do." The retirees who had retired, but remained working part-time, reported that they liked the combination of retirement and some limited part-time work. The most common part-time work was seasonal, such as retail at the holidays. The remaining retirees working full-time were an interesting group with all of them pushing back against the traditional view of retirement at age 65. Marcus summed it up for many of them when he said "What is the magic at age 65? I plan to work until I no longer want to. I may never retire."

Jay is a good example of a retiree who is satisfied with the work factor in his retirement. Yes, that is me the author of this book, and I could not let this opportunity pass without telling you my story, so I literally interviewed myself. I grew up in poverty on a farm with my two brothers and six sisters. My reality was work seven days a week with little, and in most cases, no reward. It was not a choice, but rather a necessity to help support the family. I learned that hard work resulted only in more hard work with little to show for it. Things changed dramatically when I took control of my life at age 18, earned a college degree, entered the world of work, got married, and started a family. Hard work was rewarded in many ways, but especially financially, personally, and professionally. I retired after 40 years in a public service education job because I had reached the maximum benefit in my pension, and within a week was working in my current private sector sales job. It did not happen by chance. It was planned. I knew that it was the right retirement for me after researching my options and talking to plenty of people. Work remains an important part of my identity, and I have been able to successfully balance it with my personal life. Of course, my retired friends do not understand why I am not fully retired like them and they think that it is all about the money. Nothing could be further from the truth. Even with a full-time job, I have been able to write two books and have started on a third one. Who knew that I would become an author at age 70. You will meet up with me again in chapter 18.

Retirees interviewed for the book who wanted a more rewarding retirement associated with the work factor were in almost complete agreement about their dissatisfaction at having to return to work after they had retired. In most cases, they had miscalculated their retirement income in the haste to retire, and realized when their pension checks started coming in that they were short of money and needed to find extra income or begin to withdraw funds from their savings. In a few cases, it was due to unexpected expenses, usually related to medical problems. Their decision to work part-time was driven by financial necessity, not free choice. What a devastating situation in which they found themselves, to have finally stopped working only to have to start working again. Among the most common complaints about their part-time work were that it did not create enough income to compensate for their time and that it did not fit their vision of a rewarding job. Sadly, it came down to any job was better than no job.

Martin is a good example of a retiree who wants a more rewarding retirement associated with the work factor. He retired at age 62 and filed for Social Security benefits at that time. Within a brief six months, he realized that his monthly bills exceeded his monthly income—not by a lot, but enough to warrant concern. He reluctantly returned to part-time work, but found that the income was far less than he expected even before taxes. He was considering returning to work full-time at the time of the interview. In a moment of sincerity, he said "I gave up so much for so little. I should have never stopped working."

In summary, retirees interviewed for the book who were satisfied with their retirement reported the work choices of retirement and no work, phase in retirement-phase out work, and retirement with some work as represented by the following figure. Continued work without retirement is not addressed in establishing a retirement goal because it is essentially no retirement. The reader is encouraged to create a short- or long-term retirement goal in one or more of these areas, if determined to be appropriate after self-reflection, by taking the following steps.

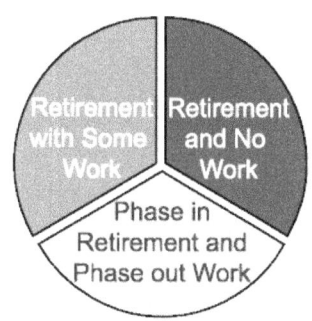

Suggested Topics for Creating a
Work Retirement Goal

- ☐ Review and reflect on the information contained in the chapter.

- ☐ Refer back to the detailed information about the work factor contained in *Discover the Right Retirement for You* if you need to and have not already done so.

- ☐ Complete the SMART goal worksheet and compare *My Description of What is Now* with *My Description of What Will Be.*

- ☐ Create a short- or long-term SMART goal as appropriate.

- ☐ Select specific strategies to successfully accomplish the goal and implement them.

- ☐ Revisit the process as often as necessary, as you accomplish each goal or conditions change.

SMART Goal Worksheet

Domain: *Wealth*   Factor: *Work*

Directions: Complete *My Description of What Is Now* and *My Description of What Will Be*. If they match there is nothing to do. If they do not match create a short- or long-term SMART goal including specific strategies to accomplish the goal.

My Description of What Is Now	My Description of What Will Be

SMART Goal
Specific – Measurable – Achievable – Realistic – Timely

I will _____ by _____ as measured by _____.
      Insert Goal   Insert Date   Insert Measurement

Strategies to Accomplish the SMART Goal

Strategy 1. _____
Strategy 2. _____
Strategy 3. _____

SMART Goal Worksheet (Example 2)

Domain: WEALTH   Factor: SAVINGS

Directions: Complete *My Description of What Is Now* and *My Description of What Will Be*. If they match there is nothing to do. If they do not match create a short- or long-term SMART goal including specific strategies to accomplish the goal.

My Description of What Is Now	My Description of What Will Be
I brought a modest savings account of $1,500 into my retirement as a rainy day fund, but have not been able to increase that amount no matter how hard I try. I have not been able to decrease my discretionary spending especially since I enjoy to shop and I have the time to do so. As a result my savings account remains low while my credit card debt continues to grow. I am worried that my car will need some major repair soon, but that I will not have the money to do it so more credit card debt.	I want to feel more financially secure that I will be able to pay for any emergency expenditures from my rainy day fund. I also want to be able to continue to do some shopping, but within reasonable limits. I have reviewed my monthly budget and know that I spend about $200 per month on many discretionary purchases which I do not really need. It is reasonable to assume that I can save $150 per month for an annual total of $1,800 which more than doubles my rainy fund the first year.

SMART Goal

Specific – Measurable – Achievable – Realistic – Timely

I will <u>increase my savings by $150 each month</u> by <u>June 2022</u> as measured by <u>a monthly bank statement</u>.

      Insert Goal   Insert Date   Insert Measurement

Strategies to Accomplish the SMART Goal

Strategy 1. Reduce discretionary shopping trips from 4x per month to 1x per month.

Strategy 2. Put $50 in a savings account envelop 3x per month in place of each shopping trip.

Strategy 3. Deposit the money each month and ask for a printed bank statement.

SMART Goal Tracking Sheet for the WEALTH Domain

Factor	SMART Goal	Start Date	Complete Date

Self Domain

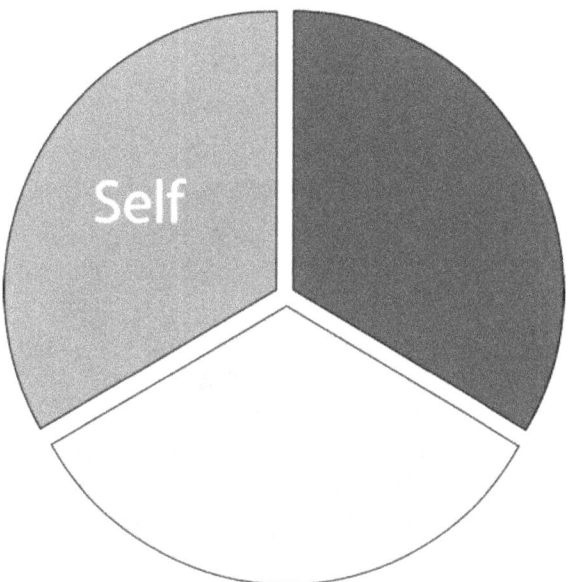

The Self Domain is concerned with how the individual perceives their self especially in relation to family, friends and others close to them. It includes the six factors of beliefs, values, interests, self-image, family, and goals. The goal is to achieve and maintain a positive perspective about one's self during the working years, as well as into and throughout retirement regardless of the number of years.

Self Factors

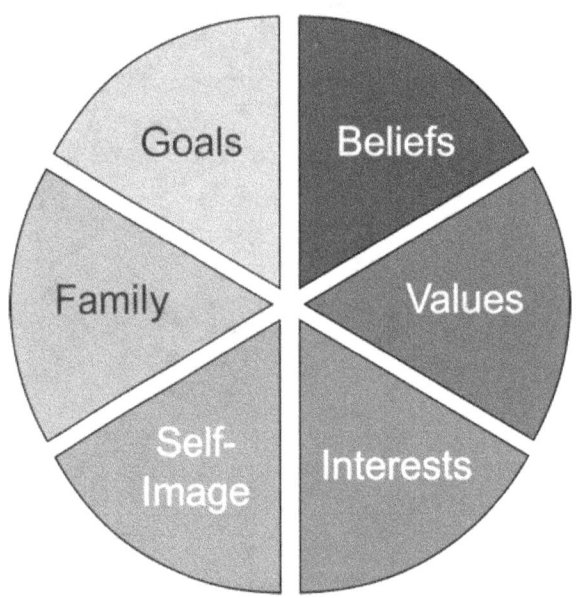

Chapter 13
BELIEFS

*In the end it's not the years in your life that count;
it's the life in your years.*
Abraham Lincoln

The following is a summary of the beliefs factor, which was first introduced in *Discover the Right Retirement for You*. The reader may choose to use this summary or review the complete description in that book to create and complete your short- and long-term retirement goals for the beliefs factor.

A belief is an idea that is accepted and acted upon as true, whether or not it is validated by facts. It is important to differentiate beliefs based upon facts from beliefs based upon misinformation, which are referred to as misbeliefs. There are four retirement misbeliefs. First, that retirement is not affected by the social interactions that the individual has at home and work. Second, that retirement is defined by a complete cessation of work. Third, that retirement is about the retiree, not family and friends who may also be affected by the decision. And lastly, that retirement looks pretty much the same for everyone.

Fundamental beliefs are developed at an early age through interactions with your family and added to and expanded upon as you live your life. Some beliefs are negative and hinder your ability to grow as a person. Other beliefs are positive and help you become the person you want to be. Bobby Hoffman has identified and described the five most powerful self-beliefs that drive daily human behavior. [31]

The first self-belief is the amount of control you have over your own destiny. If you have a strong external control focus, you believe that your destiny is not under your control and that things happen to you because of fate, luck, or other conditions that you cannot influence. A person who has a strong external control focus is very susceptible to misbeliefs. If you have a strong internal control focus, you believe that things happen because you make them happen. A person with a strong internal control focus is less susceptible to misbeliefs.

The second self-belief is competence, or your ability to get the results you want based upon your ability and skill. If you believe that you have the ability and skill to get something done, you are more likely to attempt a task and persist at it until it is completed. If you believe you do not have the ability or skill to get something done, you are more likely to avoid a task or not see it through to its completion.

The third self-belief is the degree of value you place upon the results of your efforts. There are two types of values. Intrinsic value is how you feel inside about what you do and the results you obtain. An example of intrinsic value is the self-satisfaction you get from successfully completing a job promotion examination with a passing grade. It just feels good. Extrinsic value is how those around you value what you do and what usefulness it has to you and them. An example of extrinsic value is the job promotion you receive as a result of the passing grade you obtained on the job performance examination previously mentioned. You invest significant effort in a task of high value, and little or no effort in a task of low value.

The fourth self-belief is the reason why you pursue goals. Most people acknowledge the importance of setting goals in general as a way to guide their life journey, but struggle with having a specific purpose for their goals. If the reason for pursuing a goal is compelling enough, you will accomplish the goal regardless of the obstacles you have to overcome.

And lastly, there is a self-belief about the reasons for acquiring knowledge. There are two types of knowledge. Esoteric knowledge is defined as the knowledge that is specific and unique to you and which you may or may not wish to share with others. General knowledge is defined as the knowledge that is held by most people and which you may or may not wish to acquire from them. There are also two approaches to acquiring knowledge. If you have a fixed notion of knowledge, you believe that there is one right way to do something. Conversely, if you have a flexible notion of knowledge, you believe there are many ways in which to accomplish something.

The power of your beliefs to encourage you, and in some instances your misbeliefs to discourage you, cannot be emphasized enough. Retirees interviewed for the book who were satisfied with the beliefs factor of their retirement confirmed that they had at least the three essential self-beliefs of control over their own destiny, confidence in their competence to get things done, and security in the knowledge they had acquired. They often spoke of making things happen during retirement because there was no one to tell them what to do so they had to create their own retirement reality. This was clearly an expression of a strong internal control focus. They also spoke about the belief in their ability to get things done with less likelihood of task avoidance. A number of them spoke about taking the time to learn to do something if they did not initially feel that they had the skill to do it, and then applying that new knowledge to resolve a problem. This was clearly an expression of a healthy feeling of competence. And lastly, they spoke about becoming more flexible as they grew older that they described as finding new ways to get things done. What a new twist on the old adage "You can't teach an old dog new tricks." This was clearly an expression of the flexible notion of knowledge, in which there are many ways to accomplish something.

Simon is a good example of a retiree who is satisfied with the beliefs factor in his retirement. He shared that in his job he was always stressed out because his boss was a very top-down manager who wanted everything done his way, leaving little opportunity for alternative solutions or suggestions for efficiency improvement. It was always the company way, and he occasionally avoided tasks in which he felt less confident for fear of failing or at least disappointing his boss. Simon said all that changed when he retired. He described himself as being free from his former boss and in charge of his daily routine, and by extension, in charge of his retirement in general. What was of special interest was his feeling of being able to take the time to work through daily challenges by acquiring knowledge and exploring alternate possibilities. His most noteworthy accomplishment to date was "I was able to change the faucets on the sink in the bathroom after reading up about it on Google. I did it all by myself. It was so simple and I saved a lot of money. Do you know how much a plumber makes? If I had known it a long time ago, I probably would have become one [a plumber]."

Retirees interviewed for the book who wanted a more rewarding retirement associated with their beliefs described a very different set of beliefs. The majority of them reported that they did not feel in control of their daily routine or their retirement in general, and they did not feel confident that they could make things happen. There was an almost complete lack of inquiry to gain new knowledge, with at least one of them saying "I have done it [banking] the same way for fifty years, and I am not about to change now." With the absence of the three essential self-beliefs, there was no chance these retirees would experience the remaining two self-beliefs of the value placed upon the results of their efforts and the reason for pursuing any goals at all. In essence, these retirees had had no essential beliefs to drive their daily behavior.

Connie is a good example of a retiree who wants a more rewarding retirement associated with her beliefs. She described her decision to retire as "I felt forced to retire because I could no longer stand my job." What an unhappy example of someone who had a strong external control focus and believed that she had no influence on either her work situation or retirement. She brought this same external focus into her retirement, with frequent examples of how others in her life were causing her to be inconvenienced by imposing their preferences on her, such as when to go shopping and to what stores. She gave no hint of asserting herself but rather, just lamented it. To make her retirement more rewarding, her first step will need to be to focus on her beliefs, especially control over her own destiny, and then concentrate on her confidence to get things done and security in the knowledge she acquires. She was far from this at the time of the interview.

In summary, retirees interviewed for the book who were satisfied with their retirement frequently reported the self-beliefs of control over their own destiny, confidence in their competence to get things done, and security in the knowledge they had acquired as represented in the following figure. The reader is encouraged to create a short- or long-term retirement goal in one or more of these areas, if determined to be appropriate following self-reflection, by taking the following steps.

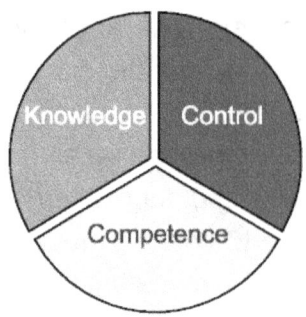

Suggested Topics for Creating a
Beliefs Retirement Goal

- ☐ Review and reflect on the information contained in this chapter.

- ☐ Refer back to the detailed information about the beliefs factor contained in *Discover the Right Retirement for You* if you need to and have not already done so.

- ☐ Complete the SMART goal worksheet and compare *My Description of What Is Now* with *My Description of What Will Be.*

- ☐ Create a short- or long-term SMART goal as appropriate.

- ☐ Select specific strategies to successfully accomplish the goal and implement them.

- ☐ Revisit the process as often as necessary, as you accomplish each goal or conditions change.

SMART Goal Worksheet

Domain: *Self* **Factor:** *Beliefs*

Directions: Complete *My Description of What Is Now* and *My Description of What Will Be*. If they match there is nothing to do. If they do not match create a short- or long-term SMART goal including specific strategies to accomplish the goal.

My Description of What Is Now	My Description of What Will Be

SMART Goal
Specific – Measurable – Achievable – Realistic – Timely

I will _____ by _____ as measured by _____.
   Insert Goal   Insert Date   Insert Measurement

Strategies to Accomplish the SMART Goal

Strategy 1. _____
Strategy 2. _____
Strategy 3. _____

Chapter 14
VALUES

As your life changes, it takes time to recalibrate, to find your values again. You might also find that retirement is the time when you stretch out and find your potential.
Sid Miramontes

The following is a summary of the values factor, which was first introduced in *Discover the Right Retirement for You*. The reader may choose to use this summary, or review the complete description in that book, to create and complete your short- and long-term retirement goals for the values factor.

Values are ideas that are important to you, expressed through the attitudes and behaviors that motivate you and guide your decisions. They are universal in that they are frequently shared among the members of the community of which you are also a member, starting at the level of the family and ending at the level of the world society. Values help shape a community by identifying what is good and bad, right and wrong, and the like. Values often suggest how community members should behave under certain circumstances, but they do not require them to do so. The community puts values into action through rewards, sanctions, and punishment. Community members are rewarded when they observe and uphold its values. They are sanctioned, or threatened with punishment, if they consider violating its values. And lastly, they are punished when they actually violate its values. In order for something to be a value, it must start as a belief that is related to an idea that has particular worth to you.

The Immigration Advisory Authority in Auckland, New Zealand, has proposed a model for the interaction of beliefs, values, attitudes, and behaviors by which earlier components, such as beliefs, affect later components, such as values, in a hierarchical fashion. Beliefs are ideas that you accept and act upon as true, whether or not they are validated by facts. Beliefs give rise to values, which are core feelings that are important to you and which the community of which you are a member hold in high regard. Values give rise to attitudes, which are a way of thinking or feeling about someone or something that is reflected in your actions. And lastly, attitudes give rise to behaviors, which are the actions you take toward others or situations. [32]

Not everyone has a well-defined set of values, or if they do, the strength of their values is tested on a regular basis. Andrew Blackman describes four barriers that you have to overcome to be able to clearly define and live by your values. [33] The first barrier is not knowing what your values are. The second barrier is lack of clarity about your values. The third barrier is lack of reconciliation, or the making of two things compatible, when your values conflict with those of the community of which you are a member. The fourth barrier is also a lack of reconciliation with your values when they conflict in a specific situation.

Paul Chernyak has developed a process by which you can discover your values and incorporate them into your life and work. [34] The process includes the three steps of discovering your values, assessing your value alignment, and incorporating your values into your life and work. The five most frequently identified values are those related to your family, relationships, productivity, life events, and culture.

The first value is family. Family values, sometimes referred to as familial values, are traditional or cultural values that pertain to the family structure, function, roles, beliefs, attitudes, and ideals that provide a foundation of protection, guidance, and support. They are the glue that holds a family together in the good and bad times across generations. The second value is relationships. A relationship is the way in which two or more concepts, objects, or people are connected or the state of being connected. The third value is productivity. Productivity is the output that is created when you apply yourself in order to achieve a goal. The fourth value is life events. Life events are those which are so significant that they have a profound effect on you. They are often referred to as life-changing events, if that effect is extreme. The last value is culture. Culture is a set of shared values, connections, and social practices associated with a particular community and received from past generations to be passed on to future generations.

Retirees interviewed for the book who were satisfied with the values factor of their retirement expressed a well-defined set of values with plenty of clarity and elaboration during their interviews. Many of their responses matched the list of the five most frequently identified values of family, relationships, productivity, life events, and culture. The entire list of responses was far more extensive than this, but the consistency of responses with the list of five was noteworthy. There was a particularly strong correlation between family and life events, especially as they related to the birth of new family members and the death of aged family members. This theme of generational renewal and passage was often repeated, with many statements about the preservation of family values and culture.

You first met Anthony in chapter 7. He is a good example of a retiree who is satisfied with the values factor in his retirement. He spoke extensively about his family, which is multigenerational and living in the same home for both financial reasons and the caregiver needs of the aged family members. He described his ethnic background and that of his family as European, specifically Italian. He expressed pride that the family was living in a multigenerational household and said "We [my wife and myself] would not have it any other way." Relatively minor inconveniences, such as limited personal space, busy schedules, and the like, were far outweighed by the benefits of holidays rich in culture and traditions, mentoring of younger family members by older family members, and the like. When asked if he could change anything, he responded "Not really. It is a way of life, our way of life, and I want our children to learn from what is happening in our family and eventually take care of us [my wife and myself] just like we do for our parents and grandparents." Anthony's values were extremely important to him and his family, and were expressed through his attitudes and behaviors just like that described at the beginning of the chapter.

Retirees interviewed for the book who wanted a more rewarding retirement associated with their values were less clear, and definitely less enthusiastic, about their values. There did not seem to be a well-defined interaction between their beliefs, values, attitudes, and behaviors. They talked about Andrew Blackman's barriers described earlier in the chapter in their own words, but it was clear they were talking about them without knowing the actual terms. The first two barriers, not knowing what their values were and not having clarity about their values, were consistently present. A few of these retirees were given an expanded interview to explore the remaining two barriers, lack of reconciliation of values when they conflict with those of the community and lack of reconciliation of values when they conflict in a specific situation. None of the retirees interviewed were successful in responding to both of these reconciliations when presented with "what would you do if" scenarios.

Stephen is a good example of a retiree who wants a more rewarding retirement associated with his values. His interview responses were very general and it was unclear if he even knew under what values he operated on a daily basis. He was presented with the Immigration Advisory Authority model described earlier in the chapter with examples of each of the components of beliefs, values, attitudes, and behaviors. When presented with the values reconciliation scenarios, he was unable to make any meaningful connections. It should be noted that this occurred during a brief interview session and it was not expected that he would be completely successful, but the complete absence of any meaning connections was surprising. Stephen has a lot of work to do with his values if he expects to be successful during retirement with this factor.

In summary, retirees interviewed for the book who were satisfied with their retirement frequently reported that they had values, attitudes, and behaviors as represented by the following figure. The reader is encouraged to create a short- or long-term retirement goal in one or more of these areas, if determined to be appropriate following your self-reflection, by taking the following steps.

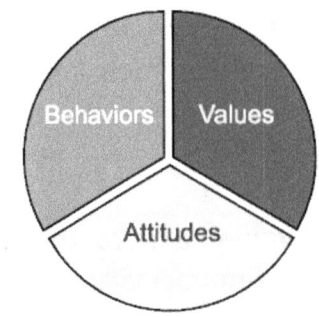

Suggested Topics for Creating a
Values Retirement Goal

☐ Review and reflect on the information contained in this chapter.

☐ Refer back to the detailed information about the values factor contained in *Discover the Right Retirement for You* if you need to and have not already done so.

☐ Complete the SMART goal worksheet and compare *My Description of What Is Now* with *My Description of What Will Be.*

☐ Create a short- or long-term SMART goal as appropriate.

☐ Select specific strategies to successfully accomplish the goal and implement them.

☐ Revisit the process as often as necessary, as you accomplish each goal or conditions change.

SMART Goal Worksheet

Domain: *Self*   Factor: *Values*

Directions: Complete *My Description of What Is Now* and *My Description of What Will Be*. If they match there is nothing to do. If they do not match create a short- or long-term SMART goal including specific strategies to accomplish the goal.

My Description of What Is Now	My Description of What Will Be

SMART Goal
Specific – Measurable – Achievable – Realistic – Timely

I will _____ by _____ as measured by _____.
         Insert Goal   Insert Date   Insert Measurement

Strategies to Accomplish the SMART Goal

Strategy 1. _____
Strategy 2. _____
Strategy 3. _____

Values ∞ 113

Chapter 15
INTERESTS

Retirement is a time to do what you want to do, when you want to do it, where you want to do it, and how you want to do it.
Catherine Pulsifer

The following is a summary of the interests factor, which was first introduced in *Discover the Right Retirement for You.* The reader may choose to use this summary, or review the complete description in that book, to create and complete your short- and long-term retirement goals for the interests factor.

Human beings are inherently curious and display that curiosity through interests. An interest is the curiosity you have about a particular thing. It can best be described as a thought-based feeling for something that usually does not require much physical effort. You can have as few as no interests, although that is highly unlikely, or any number of interests, which is the usual situation.

An interest can be either casual or committed. A casual interest is usually superficial and lasts for a short time before fading away once your curiosity has been satisfied. It can best be summed up by the statement "I have had enough of this." A committed interest is usually more intense and lasts for an extended time, seldom fading away because your curiosity is never satisfied. It can best be summed up by the statement "I cannot get enough of this."

A hobby is defined as an activity undertaken by a person for enjoyment or relaxation. It can best be described as an action done to something for ether leisure, which usually requires less physical effort, or for recreation, which usually requires more physical effort. Hobbies can require a significant amount of time and money.

It was anticipated that workers and retirees interviewed for *Discover the Right Retirement for You* would have had different levels of the commitment of time and money to their hobbies, with retirees being able to commit more time and money than workers. This was not the reality reported during their interviews. It was also of interest that there was no significant difference between workers and retirees when it came to the commitment of money. Workers reported that they anticipated increasing the money commitment to their hobbies once they retired. However, retirees reported that they had not done so for a number of reasons, including the need to reduce retirement budgets in order to maintain their overall standard of living.

A committed interest, and especially a hobby, takes time and money. The more hobbies you have, the more time and money you need. This investment should be weighed against the enjoyment and satisfaction you get from your hobby. A few workers and retirees interviewed for *Discover the Right Retirement for You* reported they had a number of committed interests and hobbies. In every situation, they reported they liked all of their hobbies but were unhappy for a number of reasons. First, they could not devote enough time to all of their hobbies, so each one was less enjoyable than it could have been. Second, they could not devote enough time to any particular one of their hobbies to really get into it. Third, they felt conflicted as to which hobbies to keep and which ones to eliminate. And lastly, the expense for one hobby was multiplied by the total number of hobbies they had, which increased the expenses charged against their retirement budget. It is recommended that you start one hobby and become the best you can at that hobby before considering adding another one. Should you want to start a second hobby, try to balance them so one is a leisure hobby and one is a recreational hobby.

Retirees interviewed for the book who were satisfied with the interests factor of their retirement consistently reported that they had many committed interests and that retirement had provided them with the opportunity to pursue these interests in depth. It was evident that their retirement provided them with the time to do so. Approximately 80 percent reported that they had increased the amount of time they spent on their identified hobbies, but they still had money issues which limited a fuller participation. It was noteworthy that about 50 percent of the retirees identified both a recreational and leisure hobby. It was even more interesting that almost all of them had increased the amount of time they spent on their leisure hobby in retirement while maintaining about the same amount of time on their recreational hobby as they spent before retirement. When asked about this difference, the frequent response was that their leisure hobby, such as reading, was easier to extend than their recreational hobby, such as running.

Joseph is a good example of a retiree who is satisfied with the interests factor in his retirement. He had two hobbies before retirement. He was a regular runner who would do five miles every day after work and on weekends. He maintained this running routine in retirement, but did not increase the number of miles even though he had the time to do so. When asked about this, he said "I like to run to clear my head and five miles is what I need to do that. I am not preparing to do a marathon or anything like that. That is of no interest to me." He was also an avid reader of forensic crime novels before retirement. He maintained this reading routine in retirement, but dramatically increased the number of novels he was reading, as well as branching off into how to forensic police investigation techniques literature. When asked about this, he said "I find this stuff [forensic crime investigation] fascinating and can't get enough of it. I sometimes regret not thinking about it as a job, but I had already been working for many years before I came across it, and by then it was too late to remake myself and start a different career." When asked if he would consider adding a leisure or recreational hobby, Joseph was clear that he liked what he was doing and did not want to do "… too many things all at once, which would take away from the enjoyment that I currently have with running and reading."

Retirees interviewed for the book who wanted a more rewarding retirement associated with their interests were almost equally divided between those who had few, if any hobbies, and those who had too many hobbies. Those who had few, if any hobbies, frequently said that they were still trying to find a hobby that interested them. This sounded reasonable, except that many of them were well beyond ten years into their retirement, and they were still trying to decide about a hobby. Ten years had already passed without a decision, and possibly another ten would pass in the same manner. Those who had too many hobbies were experiencing the frustrations of not having enough time to devote to all of them, not being able to really get in depth with a particular hobby, being conflicted as to which hobbies to keep and which to eliminate, and not being able to pay for everything they wanted to do. Even the thought of speculating about which hobbies they might want to consider eliminating was met with resistance during the interviews because they had no process by which to make such a decision.

Rebecca is a good example of a retiree who wants a more rewarding retirement associated with her interests. She reported that she has a crafts room during the interview and that doing crafts was her hobby. So far the interview was going well, but then she was asked what type of crafts she did. Her response of "… a little bit of this and a little bit of that …" was very telling. She could not describe a specific type of craft in which she was particularly interested. She expressed many of the same frustrations with those who had too many hobbies mentioned in the previous paragraph. The interview ended with Rebecca acknowledging that she had too many undefined crafts and she should do something about eliminating some of them. It is noteworthy that in a subsequent telephone interview with her before this book was finalized for publication, she said she had started to clean up her crafts room and was trying to decide if she was going to keep all of the materials or give some of them to others who might have an interest. This was a good first step in a long journey.

In summary, retirees interviewed for the book who were satisfied with their retirement consistently reported that they had a number of interests, including a variety of leisure and recreational hobbies, to which they made a personal, time, and financial commitment as represented by the following figure. The reader is encouraged to create a short- or long-term retirement goal in one or more of these areas, if determined appropriate following your self-reflection, by taking the following steps.

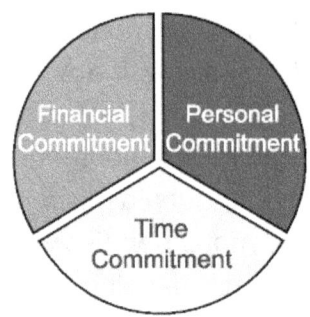

Suggested Topics for Creating an
Interests Retirement Goal

- ☐ Review and reflect on the information contained in the chapter.

- ☐ Refer back to the detailed information about the interests factor contained in *Discover the Right Retirement for You* if you need to and have not already done so.

- ☐ Complete the SMART goal worksheet and compare *My Description of What Is Now* with *My Description of What Will Be*.

- ☐ Create a short- or long-term SMART goal as appropriate.

- ☐ Select specific strategies to successfully accomplish the goal and implement them.

- ☐ Revisit the process as often as necessary, as you accomplish each goal or conditions change.

SMART Goal Worksheet

Domain: *Self*   **Factor:** *Interests*

Directions: Complete *My Description of What Is Now* and *My Description of What Will Be*. If they match there is nothing to do. If they do not match create a short- or long-term SMART goal including specific strategies to accomplish the goal.

My Description of What Is Now	My Description of What Will Be

SMART Goal
Specific – Measurable – Achievable – Realistic – Timely

I will _____ by _____ as measured by _____.
     Insert Goal   *Insert Date*   *Insert Measurement*

Strategies to Accomplish the SMART Goal

Strategy 1. _____
Strategy 2. _____
Strategy 3. _____

Chapter 16
SELF-IMAGE

*Never be bullied into silence. Never let yourself to be made a victim.
Accept no one's definition of your life, but define yourself.*
Harvey Fierstein

The following is a summary of the self-image factor, which was first introduced in *Discover the Right Retirement for You*. The reader may choose to use this summary, or review the complete description in that book, to create and complete your short- and long-term retirement goals for the self-image factor.

Self-image is a mental picture of how you perceive yourself and includes physical, psychological, and personal characteristics and traits. It is based on objective, or fact-driven assessments, such as height, weight, and the like. It is also based on subjective, or opinion-driven assessments, such as being friendly, generous, and the like. Self-image can be quite different from how the world sees you. Some people who outwardly seem to have it all, such as good looks, financial success, and the like, may have a negative self-image. Conversely, some people who face many life struggles, such as medical conditions, financial problems, and the like, may have a positive self-image. It is important that your self-image be both positive and realistic. Having a self-image that is unrealistic can be a drawback, regardless of whether that self-image is positive or negative. Having too positive a self-image can foster feelings of arrogance and entitlement. Having too negative a self-image can foster feelings of helplessness and despair. Lastly, self-image is based upon your perceptions and may, or may not, be based in reality.

It is important to understand what perception is because most of your self-image is based on your perceptions. Perception is both a physical and psychological process which occurs simultaneously. The physical process is the recognition that sensory information is coming into your brain and the psychological process is the interpretation of that information. Your perceptions do not equal your reality, but your perceptions become your reality because you act upon them as if they were the real world. Put in a different way, perception is an "inside the mind" creation of what you think you are experiencing, and reality is an "outside the mind" occurrence of the actual physical things happening around you.

Your perceptions are further affected by physiological, psychological, and social influences. Physiological influences relate to how we individually and uniquely process incoming information. For example, two people may differ significantly about the comfort of the temperature in a room even if it is within acceptable limits. One person thinks that 76 degrees is too cold, while the other person thinks that it is too hot. Psychological influences relate to the mental state we are in when we process the incoming sensory information. If we are in a positive mood, the information would be processed in a different way than if we were in a negative mood. For example, two people both find a $10 bill on the ground. The person in a positive mood may respond with "I am lucky to find this money," while the person in a negative mood might respond with "I wish it had been more money." And lastly, social influences relate to the context in which we process the information based upon our ethnic background, family experiences, and the like. For example, two people may differ significantly as to their food choices at a buffet table based upon the type of food with which they grew up.

Self-image is intertwined with self-esteem and self-confidence. Self-esteem is how you feel about your own worth. Self-confidence is how you feel about your own knowledge, judgment, and abilities. The importance of a positive self-image cannot be overstated because it affects your thinking, behavior, and relationships. Put in a different way, what we think directs our behaviors, which affect our relationships with others. This is achieved through a feedback loop, which is commonly referred to as the cycle of influence. A feedback loop is a closed system in which portions of the output are inserted back into the system as input. The cycle of influence feeds the results of life events and experiences, as well as personal relationships and interactions, into a person's self-image, which in turn structures the way in which the person approaches the next events and relationships. The feedback loop continues indefinitely through the person's lifetime. [35] A positive self-image encourages you to recognize your strengths and potential while being realistic about your weaknesses and limitations. A negative self-image encourages you to focus on your weaknesses and faults while exaggerating your failures and imperfections. The healthy choice is a positive self-image.

There are a number of actions you can take to improve your self-image. First, take stock of the positive qualities that reside within you. Choose the one that best represents who you are and make it the North Star of your character. Second, speak kindly to yourself. Monitor your self-talk and increase the positive thoughts while you decrease the negative thoughts. No one can be harder on you than yourself. And lastly, reflect well on others. Share your positive qualities with others and add value to their lives. [36]

Retirees interviewed for the book who were satisfied with the self-image factor of their retirement gave responses that expressed a positive self-image based upon both objective and subjective information. Their examples supported the idea that they had a self-image that was also realistic and closely matched the world around them. Positive self-esteem (how they felt about their own worth) and positive self-confidence (how they felt about their own knowledge, judgment, and abilities) were always present when there was a positive self-image. The most frequent response when asked about the self-image factor was "I feel good about myself," or some version thereof.

Rhonda is a good example of a retiree who is satisfied with her self-image in her retirement. She presented a well-articulated description of herself and how she felt about her image as perceived by others around her. Both responses seemed positive and realistic. When asked how she felt about the perceptions of her by others around her, she said "I genuinely think people see me as confident and positive. I like who I am and think they do, too." It was interesting that she spoke a lot about what she called her "me speech" when she was confronted with a problem. Her "me speech" is what she said to herself in her mind which she called her "inside voice," and what she said to herself out load which she called her "outside voice." Rhonda reported that sometimes she used her "inside voice" when there were others around her, but she also used her "outside voice" when she would go for a walk to think things through. She confessed that "I tend to mumble, but sometimes I need to just talk to myself. It gets me to where I need to be."

Retirees interviewed for the book who wanted a more rewarding retirement associated with their self-image stood out in stark contrast for the self-image factor from the retirees who were satisfied with their retirement. It was easy to identify these retirees. In every instance, the trifecta of negative self-image, self-esteem, and self-confidence was evident. It was how they talked and what they said that confirmed the initial impressions. As described earlier in the chapter, their negative self-image encouraged them to focus on their weaknesses and faults while exaggerating their failures and imperfections. One consistent and curious artifact was what I came to call the "qualifier." Almost every positive statement, no matter how small or inconsequential, was followed by some other negative qualifying statement which turned the good to the bad, the positive to the negative, the happy to the sad, and the like.

Marta is a good example of a retiree who wants a more rewarding retirement associated with her self-image. She was not able to provide any objective information about how she was perceived by those around her, but she did provide a limited amount of subjective information. The perception she described of herself was that of a timid and socially uncomfortable person who shied away from social encounters, always preferring to be near, but not in the middle of the action. The interview was uncomfortable for both Marta and the interviewer and at times could be described as painful as she explained always being on the outside, but wanting to be on the inside. The frequent use of the demonstrative term of "always" also provided a hint as to how negative was her self-image. Two statements using the term "always" stood out during the interview as exemplary of her negative self-image. When asked about how others around her at work thought about her, she said "I always feel like I am not part of the group." When asked about how others in her family thought about her, she said "I always feel like I am not really an important part of my family." Marta's negative self-image was part of the more complicated problem of low self-esteem and lack of self-confidence.

In summary, retirees interviewed for the book who were satisfied with their retirement had a positive self-image associated with positive self-esteem and self-confidence as represented by the following figure. The reader is encouraged to create a short- or long-term retirement goal in one or more of these areas, if determined to be appropriate following your self-reflection, by taking the following steps.

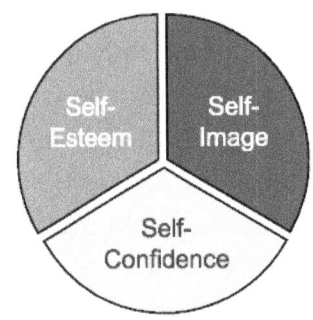

Suggested Topics for Creating a
Self-Image Retirement Goal

- ☐ Review and reflect on the information contained in the chapter.

- ☐ Refer back to the detailed information about the self-image factor contained in *Discover the Right Retirement for You* if you need to and have not already done so.

- ☐ Complete the SMART goal worksheet and compare *My Description of What Is Now* with *My Description of What Will Be.*

- ☐ Create a short- or long-term SMART goal as appropriate.

- ☐ Select specific strategies to successfully accomplish the goal and implement them.

- ☐ Revisit the process as often as necessary, as you accomplish each goal or conditions change.

SMART Goal Worksheet

Domain: *Self*   Factor: *Self-Image*

Directions: Complete *My Description of What Is Now* and *My Description of What Will Be*. If they match there is nothing to do. If they do not match create a short- or long-term SMART goal including specific strategies to accomplish the goal.

My Description of What Is Now	My Description of What Will Be

SMART Goal

Specific – Measurable – Achievable – Realistic – Timely

I will _____ by _____ as measured by _____.
      Insert Goal   Insert Date   Insert Measurement

Strategies to Accomplish the SMART Goal

Strategy 1. _____
Strategy 2. _____
Strategy 3. _____

Chapter 17
FAMILY

In family life, love is the oil that eases friction, the cement that binds us closer together, and the music that brings harmony.
Friedrich Nietzsche

The following is a summary of the family factor, which was first introduced in *Discover the Right Retirement for You.* The reader may choose to use this summary, or review the complete description in that book, to create and complete your short- and long-term retirement goals for the family factor.

Family and friends have a significant influence on our life events, including those leading up to and following the company retirement party. This chapter of the book is devoted to these influences. The following definitions were used for this chapter to maintain consistency because there are so many configurations of family and friends. A spouse refers to your husband, wife, or partner. The immediate family refers to your children, grandchildren, brothers, and sisters. The extended family refers to your parents, grandparents, aunts, and uncles. A close friend refers to anyone with whom you have regular social interactions over extended periods of time. Co-workers and colleagues were excluded from this chapter because even though they may have a friendly relationship with you, seldom does their relationship rise to the level of a family member or close friend.

The effect your family and friends have on your retirement can best described as an overlapping set of circles radiating out from you as the retiree in the center. The most influential person is your spouse, followed in order by immediate family members, extended family members, and close friends. Each exerts their own special influence on your retirement, and as the circle expands and radiates out from you, it includes more complicated interactions. In the end, it is your retirement, although you share the experience with a lot of other folks. Retirement is truly a family affair. Making isolated retirement decisions by yourself, and making informed retirement decisions with others who may have an influence on it, are worlds apart. Planning for retirement with input from your spouse, immediate and extended family members, and close friends results in a happy and healthy retirement. Lack of such planning results in you being the only person at your "shoulda, woulda, coulda" pity party, should things not work out to your liking.

Your spouse, the person with whom you live and share everything, should be the easiest person with whom to have a pre-retirement conversation. But this is not the reality. Few married couples have such a conversation about planning for their retirement, and if they do, it is about the anticipated retirement date and its associated financial impact. After money, the next retirement concern is how it will affect a couple's marriage. Since men are typically 2.3 years older than their wives, [37] couples may fantasize about a joint retirement, but it seldom happens that way. If the couple both have careers, the husband tends to retire earlier than the wife due to the age difference and often struggles with redefining himself and his place in the marriage when he goes from breadwinner to homemaker. This often results in significant problems, with the wife experiencing the stress-related condition of Retired Husband Syndrome (RHS), which may gradually erode the marriage. [38] The husband often pressures his wife to retire early so they can do things together, but working couples going from evening and weekend activities after work to 24/7 activities with no work may be way too much togetherness. Approximately 33 percent of couples disagree on what retirement will look like even when they have a pre-retirement conversation. [39]

The retirement implications for you and your spouse, immediate and extended family members, and close friends can be described using the acronym FACTS. *F* refers to financial concerns. *A* refers to physical and psychological adjustments. *C* refers to caregiving responsibilities. *T* refers to time considerations. *S* refers to social activities.

Financial concerns are related to how many sources and how much income the individual will have in retirement. The goal is to have as many income sources as possible and as much income as needed to maintain the worker's standard of living into and throughout retirement regardless of the number of years. Retirement decisions which do not include the effect of finances related to immediate and extended family members are unrealistic. There will be a need for money for both immediate and extended family members, but for different reasons. Immediate family members, especially sons and daughters, cost money to raise until they are independent adults. The cost is increased when the grandchildren come along because there is no retirement from the family. Extended family members also cost money because of their small average Social Security benefits and pensions with increased medical costs. The financial stress may not be felt while the worker is employed, but it surely will be felt when the worker becomes a retiree on a reduced or fixed retirement income.

Physical and psychological adjustments are related to achieving and maintaining a healthy balance between body and mind into and throughout retirement regardless of the number of years. Immediate family members progress from dependence to independence with routine physical childhood problems, like the occasional broken wrist, and the like, but no long-term physical problems. Their psychological mindset is that there is a lot of living still to do and so many journeys to experience. Extended family members also experience these changes, but usually in the opposite direction. They progress from independence to more dependence due to significant and usually long-term physical problems related to aging. Their psychological mindset is that they have done a lot of living already and the journey is coming to an end. Both immediate and extended family members need support to successfully navigate these physical and psychological adjustments, but for different reasons and in different ways.

Caregiving activities go from nurturing immediate family members to nursing extended family members. The need for caregiving activities decreases as our children grow up to become independent adults. Many of these caregiving activities are nonessential, such as providing transportation to the school dance, and the like. The need for caregiving activities increases as our parents and grandparents age and become more dependent on us. Many of these caregiving activities are essential, such a providing transportation to medical appointments, and the like.

"Time [and tide] wait for no man," and so it is with immediate and extended family members. The earlier years for immediate family members are measured by birth and renewal, with a long life ahead for many of them. Time passes slowly for the youngest members of this group. The later years for extended family members are measured by death and dying, with a long life already lived. Time passes quickly for the oldest members of this group. It is important to make the most of every moment, regardless of the age.

Social activities play an important role in the development of social connectedness, situational adaptability, and social belongingness. The sandwich generation is once again called upon to facilitate these activities. The social network for immediate family members grows and expands as our children and grandchildren grow into independent adults. Conversely, the social network for extended family members decreases and shrinks as they age. This is compounded by the fact that men have fewer friends than women in general, so maintenance of supportive friendships into retirement is reduced proportionally by gender. The type of relationship is also important. Men tend to share things and women tend to share feelings. [40]

Close friends are not family, but they act as if they are by attending family functions, participating in social gatherings, sharing the happiness and grief experienced by family members, and the like. Well established patterns of interaction include combined vacations, or more frequently, movies, sporting events, dinner, and the like. Close friends tend to be close in age, and in many instances, they are childhood friends who grew up together. Few workers have any discussion with their close friends about retirement, except for the date they choose to stop work or start retirement, depending on how they perceive that date.

Retirees interviewed for the book who were satisfied with the family factor in their retirement routinely reported that they had pre-retirement conversations with at least their spouse and in many instances with immediate family members. They also reported that their retirement looked like what they had discussed with them. As was expected from previous interview responses, the retirees did not have such conversations with their immediate and extended family members or close friends. They were in agreement that it would have been beneficial to have done so.

Of interest was that they also reported that they had continued to have conversations after they retired as conditions in their retirement changed.

Leonardo is a good example of a retiree who is satisfied with the family factor of his retirement. He had several pre-retirement conversations with his wife and adult children. His wife helped him select his retirement date, which was several months beyond what he had originally planned, when she pointed out that his pension would be significantly increased if he waited an additional nine months. Leonardo said that his retirement "… was kind[a] what I thought it would be and it was a smart move to stay the extra few months to increase my pension. It was helpful to have my wife's input because my retirement looks like what we talked about. No surprises for either of us."

Retirees interviewed for the book who wanted a more rewarding retirement associated with their family factor looked a lot different. They made the decision to retire all about themselves with little regard for the input from their spouse, immediate and extended family members, and close friends. When asked about the absence of such input, these retirees routinely said "It's my retirement," or some version thereof. It is noteworthy that many of them complained that they were still having "I didn't know that" moments with their spouse, immediate and extended family members, and close friends well into their retirement as their individual retirement expectations collided with their collective retirement experiences.

Mitchel is a good example of a retiree who wants a more rewarding retirement associated with his family factor. He dropped the bomb on his family when he unexpectedly came home one day and told them he had given his two-week notice that he was retiring. By his own account, things moved way too quickly and he did not have the time to do the research in order make good decisions about his pension, medical coverage, and the like. During his interview he said "I should have spent some time talking to my family to get their input, because in my haste to leave my job, I made some stupid decisions that I am now dealing with in my retirement. My advice to anyone who might read your book is to start talking about retirement as early as possible and then talk to as many folks as possible."

In summary, retirees interviewed for the book who were satisfied with their retirement frequently said that they had close relationships and meaningful discussions with their spouse, immediate and extended family members, and close friends about retirement as represented by the following figure. The reader is encouraged to create a short- or long-term retirement goal in one or more of these areas, if determined to be appropriate following your self-reflection, by taking the following steps.

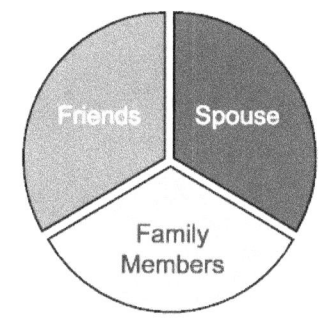

Suggested Topics for Creating a
Family Retirement Goal

☐ Review and reflect on the information contained in the chapter.

☐ Refer back to the detailed information about the family factor contained in *Discover the Right Retirement for You* if you need to and have not done so.

☐ Complete the SMART goal worksheet and compare *My Description of What Is Now* with *My Description of What Will Be.*

☐ Create a short- or long-term SMART goal as appropriate.

☐ Select specific strategies to successfully accomplish the goal and implement them.

☐ Revisit the process as often as necessary, as you accomplish each goal or conditions change.

SMART Goal Worksheet

Domain: *Self*   Factor: *Family*

Directions: Complete *My Description of What Is Now* and *My Description of What Will Be*. If they match there is nothing to do. If they do not match create a short- or long-term SMART goal including specific strategies to accomplish the goal.

My Description of What Is Now	My Description of What Will Be

SMART Goal
Specific – Measurable – Achievable – Realistic – Timely

I will _____ by _____ as measured by _____.
         Insert Goal   Insert Date   Insert Measurement

Strategies to Accomplish the SMART Goal

Strategy 1. _____
Strategy 2. _____
Strategy 3. _____

Chapter 18

GOALS

*What you get by achieving your goals is not as important
as what you become by achieving your goals.*
Henry David Thoreau

The following is a summary of the goals factor, which was first introduced in *Discover the Right Retirement for You.* The reader may choose to use this summary, or review the complete description in that book, to create and complete your short- and long-term retirement goals for the goals factor.

"All successful people have a goal. No one can get anywhere unless he knows where he wants to go and what he wants to be or do." Norman Vincent Peale sums up goals in this simple statement. However, the success of goals is more complicated than that and is based on the four P's of purpose, process, product, and plan. Purpose refers to the reason for the goal. Process refers to how the goal is created. Product refers to the actual goal. Plan refers to steps needed to reach the goal.

Andrew Carnegie, the steel magnate and philanthropist, said "If you want to be happy, set a goal that commands your thoughts, liberates your energy, and inspires your hopes." This is the essence of the goal purpose. Celestine Chua identifies several reasons for creating a goal. [41] First, many people are sleepwalking through life. Creating a goal lets you break out of auto-pilot and start living a life of your own conscious creation. Second, just working, and working toward a goal, are worlds apart. Creating a goal sets a tangible target toward which to work. Third, creating a goal gives you a laser focus on where to spend your time and energy. Fourth, creating a goal makes you accountable for reaching that goal. The ownership is on you and no one else. Fifth, creating a goal connects you with your innermost desires and dreams. The transformation from the abstract to the actual is amazing. Sixth, creating a goal helps you be the best you can be. And lastly, creating a goal ensures you get the best out of your life.

Michelangelo, artist and inventor, said, "The greatest danger for most of us isn't that we aim too high and we miss [the goal], but that it is too low and we reach it [the goal]." This is the essence of the goal process. Adam Sicinski has identified a five-step goal-setting process. [42] These steps include the following: define what you want; find congruence with your other life factors; determine the ultimate consequences of achieving the goal; identify any potential obstacles that will keep you from reaching the goal; and draw up a plan of action. Gavin Ingham has identified the most common reasons for people not setting goals. [43] These reasons include the following: surrounding ourselves with people who do not have goals; setting the wrong goals; hanging on to disappointments about previous unmet goals; fear that keeps us in our safety zone and paralyses us into inaction; and seeking immediate instead of delayed rewards.

C. S. Lewis, the prolific writer best known for his *Chronicles of Narnia* series, said "You are never too old to start another goal or to dream a new dream." This is the essence of the goal product: that is, the goal itself. Successful goal creation can be described using the acronym SMART. *S* refers to specific; *M* refers to measurable; *A* refers to achievable; *R* refers to relevant; and *T* refers to timely. A specific goal is one that includes enough detail to be well defined and unambiguous. A measurable goal is one which has criteria by which to measure the progress toward and final achievement of the goal. An achievable goal is one which is attainable given the available human and material resources. A realistic goal is one which is relevant and within reach. And lastly, a timely goal is one with a beginning and ending date.

The following example illustrates a successful SMART goal. Betty plans to retire from her current job of 25 years as an accountant with a large technology company in Silicon Valley and start an encore job as an accounting consultant. She has created the following SMART goal: "I will begin working as an accounting consultant no later than January 1, 2022, by having at least one consulting contract." The SMART goal is made up of three explicit (clearly stated) components, and two implicit (implied) related components. The explicit components include those which are specific, measurable, and timely. Betty's goal is specific because she wants to "start an encore job as an accounting consultant." It is measurable because she will have "at least one consulting contract." And it is timely because she has set the date as "no later than January 1, 2022." The implicit components include those which are realistic and achievable. Betty's goal is realistic because she has researched the local job market and knows that 67 percent of all retired accountants are working at least part-time as consultants. It is achievable because she already is an accountant and has the necessary job skills without having to retrain.

Pablo Picasso, Spanish artist, sculptor, and printmaker, said "Our goals can only be reached through the vehicle of a plan, in which we must fervently believe, and upon which we must vigorously act. There is no other route to success." This is the essence of the goal plan. Just like a SMART goal, the plan to achieve the goal must be specific. It must include the five W's of who, what when, where, and why. And just like a SMART goal, the plan to achieve the goal must be taken from the abstract to the actual by writing it down. The final step is the easiest, as well as the hardest – DO IT! Shawn Lim lists a number of reasons why people fail to implement their goal plans. [44] These reasons include the following: they do not have a specific goal; they have doubts about reaching the goal; they do not spend time and energy on the goal; they have goals that do not inspire them; they are not committed to the goal because they had come this far without it; they cannot focus on the goal because they are doing too many other things; they give too many excuses; and they jump from goal to goal never giving themselves time to work through the challenges inherent in the task.

Retirees interviewed for the book who were satisfied with the goals factor in their retirement actually had goals and were able to articulate them in some detail. Some were short-term goals and others were long-term goals. When asked about these goals, the frequent response was that the retirees had always lived by goals, even when they were working, and they had brought this behavior into retirement. Samuel summed it up when he said "Without goals, my retirement would be pretty empty. I have goals from the time I get up to the time I go to bed. Some are tiny, but others are quite big. I didn't stop living, I just retired." Each retiree was presented with the SMART goal process described earlier in the chapter, and all of them were interested in it for two reasons. First, some of the retirees found the SMART goal process to be useful to them in creating a structure by which they could add more specificity to their goals. Second, the remainder of them found that the SMART goal process was closely aligned with what they were currently doing, and it gave credibility and validation to their goals.

Jay is a good example of a retiree who is satisfied with the goals factor of his retirement. You first met me in Chapter 12 as the author of this book. I have lived by goals for as long as I can remember. I teach SMART goal creation as part of my curriculum at the local college. Some of my goals were planned in advance, such as saving enough money to buy my first car. This is the typical type of goal of which we are all aware. Other goals were created after an opportunity presented itself unexpectedly, such as the writing of this book. I was encouraged by family and friends to write *Create Your Own Rewarding Retirement* after the success of my first book. I created the SMART goal "I will write a book about making retirement rewarding through the creation of SMART goals by December 31, 2020, as measured by the submission of the first draft of the book to a publishing company." The SMART goal included the three explicit components that it was specific, measurable, and timely. It included the two implicit components that it was realistic because there are many authors like me out there already and that it was achievable because I had already written one book on the topic.

Retirees interviewed for the book who wanted a more rewarding retirement associated with their goals had very few goals, and if they did, the goals were extremely short-term. When asked about these goals, they were unable to articulate them in specific terms. In one instance, Molly stated "I had enough of goals when I was working. There was always some production goal to meet and it got pretty boring. I was not about to make my retirement look like that." Most of the retirees interviewed for the book did agree that some form of goals was beneficial and would give their retirement more direction. Each retiree was presented with the SMART goal process described earlier in the chapter and most of them were interested, or so they said. The rhetoric did not equal the reality. Each retiree was asked to create a short-term retirement goal using the SMART goal process and they all complied, but with very little real interest and enthusiasm. It was expected that their interest and enthusiasm would further decline once they left the interview.

Karen is a good example of a retiree who wants a more rewarding retirement associated with her goals factor. She had been retired for a number of years at the time of the interview, but she was still living as if each day was the day after she left work and began her retirement. There is a natural response to want to relax for a while and decompress from a life of work, but for most people this lasts a few days to a few weeks before they begin a life of retirement in earnest. Karen never got out of this transition time. She said that her days were fairly routine and predictable without much variation even on the weekends. Karen made a noteworthy comment that "I lose track of what day it is pretty often because they [the days] all seem to be the same." It was interesting and unexpected that unlike the retirees described in the previous paragraph, she responded actively and affirmatively when presented with the SMART goal process. As she was leaving the interview, Karen said that she would be seriously considering the creation of at least one SMART goal, and her sincerity was unquestionable. This small step may lead to a more rewarding retirement for her.

In summary, retirees interviewed for the book who were satisfied with their retirement frequently said that they had a process by which they created goals and monitored them to completion as represented by the following figure. The reader is encouraged to create a short- or long-term retirement goal in one or more of these areas, if determined to be appropriate following your self-reflection, by taking the following steps.

Suggested Topics for Creating a
Goals Retirement Goal

☐ Review and reflect on the information contained in the chapter.

☐ Refer back to the detailed information about the goals factor contained in *Discover the Right Retirement for You* if you need to and have not done so.

☐ Complete the SMART goal worksheet and compare *My Description of What Is Now* with *My Description of What Will Be.*

☐ Create a short- or long-term SMART goal as appropriate.

☐ Select specific strategies to successfully accomplish the goal and implement them.

☐ Revisit the process as often as necessary, as you accomplish each goal or conditions change.

SMART Goal Worksheet

Domain: *Self*   Factor: *Goals*

Directions: Complete *My Description of What Is Now* and *My Description of What Will Be*. If they match there is nothing to do. If they do not match create a short- or long-term SMART goal including specific strategies to accomplish the goal.

My Description of What Is Now	My Description of What Will Be

SMART Goal
Specific – Measurable – Achievable – Realistic – Timely

I will _____ by _____ as measured by _____.
         Insert Goal   Insert Date   Insert Measurement

Strategies to Accomplish the SMART Goal

Strategy 1. _____
Strategy 2. _____
Strategy 3. _____

GOALS ∞ 141

SMART Goal Worksheet (Example 3)

Domain: SELF   Factor: FAMILY

Directions: Complete *My Description of What Is Now* and *My Description of What Will Be*. If they match there is nothing to do. If they do not match create a short- or long-term SMART goal including specific strategies to accomplish the goal.

My Description of What Is Now	My Description of What Will Be
Family has always been important to me and while I was working it was difficult to balance everything between family and work. I expected things to get better once I retired and it did because the demands of work were eliminated. However, they were re-placed with an increase of family needs since I care for my elderly parents who both have significant medical problems requiring many doctor appointments. It seems as if I have less time for myself than ever before and my life feels unbalanced.	I will have a more balanced life between helping my elderly parents with things like their medical appointments and my personal time. I will have at least one day each week that is for the things I want to do and at least one evening each week that is for social activities with my friends. I will have to be flexible with the specific days and evenings, but will be able to accomplish this by proactively meeting with my parents in advance to schedule in their medical appointments.

SMART Goal

Specific – Measurable – Achievable – Realistic – Timely

I will _find some private time for myself_ by _May 2022_ as measured by _the entries in my monthly calendar_.

    Insert Goal   Insert Date   Insert Measurement

Strategies to Accomplish the SMART Goal

Strategy 1. Maintain a monthly calendar of all medical appointments for my parents.

Strategy 2. Meet with my parents weekly to schedule medical appointments at least 2 weeks in advance.

Strategy 3. Review my weekly calendar to make sure I have created time for myself.

SMART Goal Tracking Sheet for the SELF Domain

Factor	SMART Goal	Start Date	Complete Date

Conclusion

Congratulations on finishing the book. There was plenty of material to read and reflect upon as told through the stories of retirees who were satisfied with their retirement and retirees who wanted a more rewarding retirement. Even though the book is about their stories, you may have recognized yourself in many of the pages and experienced many of the same things they did. It is hoped that it has been of value to you in creating and completing your short- and long-term goals after you retire. Remember that you, and you alone, have the ability to make an ordinary retirement into an extraordinary one.

REFERENCES

1. "Eight Areas of Age-Related Change" at NIH Medline Plus Special Edition.

2. "Treadmill Walking Workout Plan for Seniors" by Wendy Bumgardner at https://www.verywellfit.com, 02/27/2018.

3. "Normal Cognitive Aging" by Caroline Harada in Clinical Geriatric Medicine, 11/01/2013.

4. "What Is Executive Functioning" by Joyce Cooper-Kahn and Laurie Dietzel at https://www.idonline.org, 2019.

5. "Toward a New Definition of Mental Health," World Psychiatry Journal, Volume 14 (2), June 2015.

6. National Mental Health Organization at https://healthylife.com, 2004.

7. "What is Emotional Health and How to Improve It" at https://healthyplace.com.

8. "Emotional Wellness Toolkit" at https://www.nih.gov.

9. "Definition of Health" at https://www.who.

10. The Social Self by Robert C. Ziller, 01/01/1973.

11. "Six Components of a Model for Workplace Spirituality" by Kent Rhodes, Graziado Business Review, Volume 9 (2), 11/02/2006.

12. "Social Security Cost of Living Adjustment (COLA)" at https://www.ssa.gov/cola.

13. "Breadwinning Mothers Are Increasingly the U.S. Norm" by Sarah Glynn, Center for American Post, 12/04/2011.

14. "What's The Largest Social Security Check Someone Can Get?" by Michelle Singletary, The Washington Post, 12/04/2017.

15. "Retirees Increasingly Depending on Social Security" by Emily Brandon, U.S. News and Report, 08/30/2011.

16. "How Work Affects Your Benefits" at https://sss.gov/pubs/EN-05-10069.pdf.

17. "The Shift from Defined Benefit to Defined Contribution Plans" by the Greenbush Financial Group LLC, 2018.

18. "What Is Compound Interest?" at Investor.gov. U.S. Securities and Exchange Commission, 09/02/2018.

19. "Tax-Deferred Retirement Account" at https://www.irs.gov/retirementplans/401k-plans.com.

20. "These Are the New HSA Limits for 2020" at https://www.cnbc.com.

21. "IRAs: Everything You Need to Know" by Dayana Yochim, Nerdwallet, 04/30/2018.

22. "FDIC Deposit Insurance FAQs," 01/31/2018.

23. "Series EE Savings Bonds" at https://www.treasurydirect.gov.

24. "Here's How Much Money Americans Have in Their Savings Accounts" by Katherine Elkins, Money, 09/13/2017.

25. "Distinguish Between Wants and Needs" by Erin Huffstetler, The Balance, 06/13/2018.

26. "Six Types of Diversification for Your Portfolio" by Isaac Presely, Investopedia, 03/28/2017.

27. "Bond Laddering Definition" by Carol Kopp, Investopedia, 01/17/2019.

28. Epic America by James Truslow Adams, 1931.

29. "Too Many Too Big Houses" by Candice Taylor, The Wall Street Journal Special Retirement Living Unit, 03/22/2019.

30. "The Five Types of People Who Never Retire: Are You One of Them?" by Maria Walters, Breadwise, 11/26/2014.

31. "The 5 Most Powerful Beliefs That Ignite Human Behavior" by Bobby Hoffman, https://www.elsevier.com, 09/16/2015.

32. "Immigration Advisory Authority Model" at https://www.iaa.govt.nz.

33. "What Are Your Personal Values? How to Define and Live by Them" by Andrew Blackman at www.business.tutsplus.com, 08/04/2018.

34. "How to Define Your Personal Values" by Paul Chernyak at www.wikihow.com, 09/18/2019.

35. "Cycle of Influence" at https://www.Destinyodyssey.com.

36. "3 Ways to Improve Your Self-Image" by John Maxwell at success.com, 09/25/2018.

37. "What's the Average Age Difference in a Couple?" by Mona Chalabi at Fivethirtyeight.com, 01/22/2015.

38. "How Retirement Affect Marriage?" at https://www.gransnet.com/relationships.

39. "When One Spouse Retires Before the Other" by Jane Bennett at Kiplinger's Personal Finance, 12/2014.

40. "How Are Men's Friendships Different from Women's?" by Ronald Riggio at Psychology Today, 10/09/2014.

41. "7 Important Reasons Why You Should Set Goals" by Celestine Chua at https://personalexcellence.

42. "Breaking Down the Five-Step Goal-Setting Process" by Adam Sicinski at blog.iqmatrix.com.

43. "7 Reasons Why People Don't Set Goals and Why You Should" by Gavin Ingham at https://recruitmentjuice.com, 04/05/2017.

44. "Top 10 Reasons Why People Fail to Reach Their Goals" by Shawn Lim at https://goalcast.com, 09/12/2016.

www.ingramcontent.com/pod-product-compliance
Lightning Source LLC
Chambersburg PA
CBHW082331220526
45470CB00008B/2467